THE BETRAYAL
OF WORK

THE BETRAYAL
OF WORK

HOW LOW-WAGE JOBS FAIL

30 MILLION AMERICANS

AND THEIR FAMILIES .

Beth Shulman

THE NEW PRESS

NEW YORK
LONDON

Published in the United States by The New Press, New York, 2003
Distributed by W. W. Norton & Company, Inc., New York

LIBRARY OF CONGRESS CATALOGING-IN-PUBLICATION DATA
Shulman, Beth.
The betrayal of work : how low-wage jobs fail 30 million Americans
and their families / Beth Shulman.
p.   cm.
Includes bibliographical references.
ISBN 1-56584-733-4
1. Wages—United States.   2. Income distribution—United States.
3. Family—Economic aspects—United States.   4. Working poor—United States.
5. Working poor—United States—Case studies.   6. United States—Economic
conditions—2001–   I. Title.
HD4975.S46 2003
331.2'3—dc21   2003043413

The New Press was established in 1990 as a not-for-profit alternative to the large, commercial publishing houses currently dominating the book publishing industry. The New Press operates in the public interest rather than for private gain, and is committed to publishing, in innovative ways, works of educational, cultural, and community value that are often deemed insufficiently profitable.

The New Press
38 Greene Street, 4th floor
New York, NY 10013
www.thenewpress.com

In the United Kingdom:
6 Salem Road
London W2 4BU

Composition by dix!

Printed in the United States of America

2   4   6   8   10   9   7   5   3

12/03

To my husband, Ernie
for his love and support

and

To Aaron
who makes every day a blessing

Is this improvement in the circumstances of the lower ranks of the people to be regarded as an advantage or as an inconveniency to the society? . . . It is but equity . . . that they who feed, cloath and lodge the whole body of the people, should have such a share of the produce of their own labour as to be themselves tolerably well fed, cloathed and lodged.

Adam Smith, *The Wealth of Nations*

You shall not abuse a needy and destitute laborer, whether a fellow countryman or a stranger in one of the communities of your land.

Deuteronomy 24:14

CONTENTS

Acknowledgments   ix
Introduction   1

CHAPTER 1   Three Workers   15

CHAPTER 2   Piling On: Why It's About More
            Than Money   25

CHAPTER 3   In the Heart of Our Economy and
            Our Lives   45

CHAPTER 4   The Demography of a Caste   69

CHAPTER 5   How Low-Wage Jobs Damage Us All   81

CHAPTER 6   An Apology for Indifference   101

CHAPTER 7   A Question of Power   117

CHAPTER 8   A Compact with Working Americans   149

Notes   185
Index   241

ACKNOWLEDGMENTS

Many people helped make this book possible. I am especially indebted to Lance Lindblom and Eric Wanner. From the very beginning, they gave me their encouragement, support, thoughtful suggestions, and their precious time. Words cannot convey my gratitude for their enormous generosity. I am also thankful to the Ford Foundation and the Russell Sage Foundation for their initial funding that allowed me to take a leave of absence and focus on this book.

From the outset, I was aided with a gifted editor, Steve Fraser. He shared my passion for this issue and helped steer me through the process with his exceptional knowledge and keen editorial skills. He kept me going in difficult times, but never failed to give me needed criticisms. I want to thank The New Press who provided me with a talented editor, Andy Hsiao, who continually pushed me to make this a better book and whose comments were enormously helpful.

My friend and colleague Jack Meyer read the manuscript in

each of its permutations and provided me with invaluable insights and assistance with technical data. His critiques provided a more balanced viewpoint. He and his colleagues at the Economic and Social Research Institute were generous with their time, for which I am very thankful. I also want to thank Andy Stern and John Wilhelm for sharing their perspectives on the labor movement and helping me with connections with workers; Richard Freeman, Larry Mishel, Jared Bernstein, and Paul Osterman, whose excellent work in this area and comments brought a clearer view of the problem; Joan Williams and Heidi Hartmann for their help on issues involving work and family; Annette Bernhardt for helping me understand the depths of the low-wage mobility problem and introducing me to some creative projects that help; Laurie Bassi for her help on training issues; Katherin Ross Phillips for her assistance in providing data on low-wage workers; Kathy Bonk and Janet Shenk, who read the final draft of the manuscript and provided helpful suggestions; members of the Domestic Strategy Group of the Aspen Institute, whose knowledge and give-and-take helped me think about these issues more creatively; Damon Silvers, who helped bring me to this point; Politics and Prose, for providing such a wonderful place to write; and to the many other people, many of whom are cited in the endnotes, who gave me their valuable time and assistance. Of course, it goes without saying, any mistakes in this book are all my own.

My deepest debt of gratitude goes to the workers who were willing to tell me their stories. They welcomed me into their homes, fed me, and shared their lives. It was an honor that I will always cherish. And to my family and friends who have heard more about this book than they wished, yet supported me at every turn.

Finally, I want to thank my husband, Ernie. He has been my greatest supporter, providing me with his love, intelligence, and editing expertise. In times of discouragement, his helpful suggestions have kept me going. And most of all I thank him for his belief in me and this book.

THE BETRAYAL
OF WORK

INTRODUCTION

As we drove down the long dirt road, the car jerked as it hit each bump. Cynthia Porter apologized for the road as if it were her fault. After more than thirty minutes, we finally passed her landlord's large house and pulled up in front of her small maroon-colored shack. It was miles from a main road. Cynthia looked embarrassed. "It's a mess," she said. The rickety wood stairs creaked as we walked up to the front door. The screen door was askew. Inside, the plywood floor was so thin that the ground could be seen below. In the next room, a toilet sank into the floor. There was no phone. A broken heater sat against the wall. The landlord refused to fix it.

Still, the few pieces of worn furniture were wiped clean and everything was in its place. On the tar paper walls were photographs of her three children and, in a minute, they came running inside from playing. Keeping their clothes clean, however, requires great effort, because Cynthia has no washing machine.

Instead, she fills her bathtub halfway and gets on her hands and knees to scrub their clothes. Then she hangs them out to dry.

Cynthia Porter is not on welfare. She works as a certified nursing assistant at a nursing home in Marian, Alabama. When Cynthia comes on duty at 11:00 P.M., she makes rounds. She checks the residents for skin tears and helps them go to the toilet or use a bedpan. She has to make sure she turns the residents every two hours or they will get bedsores, and if bedsores are left unattended, they can get so bad that you can put your fist in them.

But there aren't enough people on her shift. Often there are only two nursing assistants for forty-five residents. In addition to responding to the needs of the residents, Cynthia must also wash the wheelchairs, clean up the dining rooms, mop the floors and scrub out the refrigerator, drawers, and closets during her shift. Before she leaves, she helps the residents get dressed for breakfast.

For all of this, Cynthia makes $350 every two weeks. She is separated from her husband, who gives her no child support. The first two weeks each month she pays her $150 rent. The next two weeks, she pays her water and her electric bills. It is difficult to afford Clorox or shampoo. Ensuring that her children are fed properly is a stretch, and she is still paying off the bicycles she bought for her children last Christmas.

She can't afford a car, so she ends up paying someone to drive her the twenty-five miles to work. And there have been a few days when she couldn't find a ride. "I walked at twelve o'clock at night," she said. "I'd rather walk and be a little late than call in. I'd rather make the effort. I couldn't just sit here. I don't want to miss a day, otherwise, I might be fired." There is no public transportation that would take her to work.

I first met Cynthia at a union meeting. She had a quiet, dignified presence with her dark suit and her hair pulled back in a bun. She and twenty-five others from the nursing home—all eighty of her coworkers are African American women like her—gathered in the little brick Masonic building outside of Marian to talk about having a union. Like Cynthia, none had ever gotten a raise of more than 13 cents. Some who had been there ten years were still making $6.00 an hour. But it was the lack of respect from their employer that motivated these women. They would tell their supervisors something important about patients, but, they said, no one listened. There were no promotional opportunities either. As Cynthia said, "I knew it wouldn't improve without outside help."

And yet, despite the frustration and the difficult conditions, Cynthia beams when she talks about her job. "I like helping people," she says. "I like talking with them, and shampooing their hair. I like old people. If they are down, I can really make them feel better. The patients say nobody loves me or comes to see me. Sometimes I help the residents play dominos. Sometimes their hands shake but I hold them. It's a lot of fun for them. I tell them I love you and give them a hug. I like being a CNA. I'm doing what I want to be doing." *

---

*Because the workers I spoke with have very little power in their workplaces, they also take great risks when they simply talk about their jobs to outsiders. Therefore, I have changed their names and only identified their employers when there was no possibility of revealing their identities.

.   .   .

In 1960, Michael Harrington published a book that stirred the conscience of a nation. *The Other America* reminded a country basking in the glow of postwar prosperity that poverty was alive and well in its midst. Poverty, Harrington revealed, afflicted those invisible millions living in passed-over regions of the country and the economy—those marginalized in Appalachia, in the South, in rural America. They were caught in dying towns and industries, shunted off the main tracks of the economy into unemployment, and left to fester in idleness and despair. In a word, they were outlanders, watching as the rest of the country went to work and thrived. The nation spent the remainder of the century wrestling with this sort of poverty, expanding and then contracting the welfare state as it experimented with different ways of dealing with the problems of a population cut off from the economic mainstream. All that has changed.

True, old forms of poverty continue, and even now the country is arguing about what to do with its welfare recipients. But the great secret of America is that a vast new impoverished population has grown up in our midst. Yet these are not Americans who have been excluded from the world of work; in fact, they make up the core of much of the new economy. Indeed, our recent prosperity rests, in part, on their misery. Their poverty is not incidental to their role as workers, but derives directly from it.

They are America's super-exploited. And this is both a shame and a challenge of historic proportions. A shame because America has always honored work, yet now finds itself in the position of degrading it. A challenge because whatever one thought of

America's welfare poor, few people were making money off them. The same cannot be said of our new working poor. Corporations, corporate executives, shareholders, and American consumers are making a lot of money off of them. Thirty million Americans, one out of every four workers, makes less than $8.70 an hour. And these low-wage, no-benefit jobs translate into billions of dollars of profits, executive pay, high stock prices, and low consumer prices.

The question of poverty today is a question of both reexamining the balance of power in our society and challenging a society that eviscerates its low-wage workers. This is always a difficult prospect, but unavoidable if we are to uphold the national commitment to work and its just rewards. This is a book devoted not only to describing the dimension of poverty in the American workplace, but to exploring its roots in the imbalances of social, political, and economic power and to offering solutions to these injustices.

For several years, I have traveled the country talking with workers like Cynthia Porter. They are hardworking Americans who can't make it on their jobs. Cynthia is not unique. While the details vary, the story is repeated again and again. It is a story about workers who are the embodiment of the work ethic. It is about workers who perform tasks essential to Americans' lives, yet seem hidden from their view. It is about workers who pay their taxes and do their jobs with great dedication and care, yet get little in return. They are workers on the margin. They are America's invisible working poor.

They are nursing home workers and home health-care workers who care for our mothers and fathers, yet make so little in-

come that many qualify for food stamps. They are poultry processing workers who bone and package the chicken we eat for
our dinner, yet are not allowed to leave the line to go to the bathroom. They are retail store workers who help us in department
stores, grocery stores and convenience stores, but can't get
enough hours or benefits to support themselves without working at least two jobs. They are hotel workers who ensure that the
rooms we sleep in on our business trips and family vacations are
clean, but who have no sick days or funeral leave or vacation
time. They are janitorial workers who empty our wastebaskets
after dark but who have no child care. They are catfish workers
who process the fish we enjoy, but must work with injured wrists
from continuous motion on the line. They are 1-800 call-center
workers who answer our requests and take our orders while
under constant management surveillance. And they are child-
care workers who educate and care for our children while their
own live in poverty.

The United States has built its recent prosperity on the strain
and stress of these people. We saw in the late nineties, after
nearly a decade of economic growth, that wages increased for
these workers in areas where there was very low unemployment. These markets had forced employers to compete for workers, giving workers some ability to win improvements. But even
during the best of economic times, these workers were barely
scraping by. These record conditions have not continued. Low-
wage service workers have borne the brunt of the cutbacks in
our economy in the form of lost jobs and reductions in hours
and pay.

Much public attention is focused on moving Americans off of

welfare, and almost everywhere, it seems, there have been calls to ensure that those who receive government welfare assistance perform work. But little outrage is reserved for the over thirty million Americans who work hard every day, and yet struggle to take care of their families. Who these workers are contributes to this public indifference. A majority are female and many are minorities and immigrants. These groups historically have been forgotten, viewed as somehow less deserving or less in need of support. It is only with the plunging wages of working-class white males that some attention has been paid. The realization that those previously on welfare cannot support themselves and their families in low-wage jobs has also brought a recent awareness of the inadequacies of these jobs. Barbara Ehrenreich's excellent book, *Nickel and Dimed: On (Not) Getting By in America*, in which she tries and fails to live on the wages from these low-end jobs, generated some passing sympathy.

However, the reigning American mythology that being in a low-wage job is a temporary situation, that mobility will solve the problem, undermines such concern. But the evidence belies the myth. While some lower-wage workers will move up the ladder, most will never move into the middle class. Their children will suffer the same fate. Ignoring this reality leaves in place what Harvard economist Richard Freeman calls an "apartheid economy."

Inadequate wages are only one part of the problem. Most of these workers lack basic job benefits such as health care, sick pay, disability pay, paid vacation, and retirement. Their jobs leave little flexibility to care for a sick child or deal with an emergency at school—let alone the normal appointments and needs of everyday life. Quality child care is unaffordable for most and many nighttime shifts, forced overtime, and employer changes in schedules make it even harder to find and more expensive to obtain.

Low-wage workplaces are often physically damaging and emotionally degrading. High injury rates plague these workers. Constant surveillance, time clocks, drug testing, and rigid rules reinforce the pervasive sense that employers view them as untrustworthy. Fear is the chief motivator in these workplaces. Being five minutes late can mean the difference between having a job and not. A few minutes too long in the bathroom could mean discipline or a dock in pay. It is not surprising that with so little employer respect, these workers receive minimal training and few opportunities for input into their jobs. In fact, in most low-wage workplaces voicing one's opinion is discouraged.

Yet some argue that all of this is the inextricable consequence of "low-skill" jobs, that workers in low-wage jobs must obviously have low skills. Most economists, politicians, and the media marry the two terms as if they were inseparable. Stockbrokers who earn $150,000 a year are deemed skilled, whereas child-care workers who earn $15,000 a year are called low-skilled regardless of the difficulty or worth of what they're doing.

Low skills are also used as a synonym for less formal education. This equation is not surprising. Those who determine the dialogue of the debate are generally well-educated. They have not really looked at the skills required of these lower-wage jobs or the skills possessed by those who do these jobs. They rely instead on stereotypes.

This "low-skilled" label is a distancing device. It allows us to dismiss these workers as undeserving, somehow flawed. It allows us to justify how poorly their employers treat them. It makes it easier to blame them for their own economic plight. Undervaluing low-wage job skills, most of which involve working with people, is especially ironic in our consumer-driven, service economy. But denigration is no accident. Many low-wage jobs have historically been "women's jobs." These jobs involve nurturing, caring, and communicating with people, skills that have been historically trivialized.

Declaring these jobs "low-skilled" also warps public policy. Across the political spectrum, improving workers' skills has become the panacea for improving the living standards of these workers. In a society in awe of new computer technologies, this focus is understandable. It is easy to explain away problems by referring to a lack of technological proficiency. But this "skills" solution avoids the profoundly political question of how profits should be shared with workers. It gets employers off the hook. It also relieves the rest of us from thinking about the inequity of the rules governing relations between these workers, their employers, and our society.

Skills are not the problem, however much we might like to believe otherwise. These workers have the requisite know-how for their jobs as child-care workers, nursing home workers, poultry processors, and janitors. Of course, better education and fluency in new technologies are essential to improve job options for this and the next generation of workers. Workers should also receive training throughout their careers to have opportunities for job and social mobility. Yet, these labor-intensive industries will continue to demand large numbers of workers regardless of individual mobility, and these are the growing sectors of our economy. It is the rewards of the jobs that must be improved.

It is time we discarded the ahistorical premise that there is something about these jobs themselves that makes them "bad jobs," unchanging in what they provide to workers. Jobs are defined by institutional arrangements: labor power, market power, political power, ideology, and values. It is not the particular activities one does while on the job that determines whether a job is "good" or "bad," but rather the power to influence employers to change work conditions. As the power relationships change, the nature of jobs change.

Today's "good jobs" in large-scale manufacturing were not always good. Working in a factory is hard work. It can be dirty and unsafe. At one time, it paid poor wages and had few benefits. But factory jobs became "good" jobs in this country when employers were forced to make them so through worker power in unions. This success also forced nonunion employers to change their wage and benefit packages to compete for workers. This power, combined with earlier New Deal labor legislation, set a floor on employment standards on issues such as minimum wages, maximum hours of work, and overtime requirements. Social legislation of the late sixties and early seventies regulated workplace safety and health, equal employment opportunity, and a range of other employment conditions.

Through these two processes of collective bargaining and government regulation, wages and working conditions were significantly improved and norms were established. A uniquely private arrangement of employer-provided benefits was developed. Of course, these were not halcyon days for all American workers. The manufacturing industries that labor unions organized were predominantly made up of white males. Unions largely bypassed the service sector, except for notable exceptions in the telecommunications and the retail food industries. As a result, the social contract for hourly workers did not take root outside the large-scale manufacturing industries.

Today's low-wage workers have little labor, market, or political power. This imbalance comes from societal decisions: monetary policy that stresses fighting inflation over job creation; trade policies that fail to take into account the impact on lower-end jobs; corporate policies that have allowed CEOs nearly unfettered discretion to determine their own rewards and those of their workers; wage policies such as a minimum-wage law that has failed to keep up with inflation; labor laws that make it difficult for workers to collectively organize; and still other employment and labor laws that exclude many of the most vulnerable workers. This leaves these workers virtually powerless to change their situations. They can't give large political donations, so little attention is focused on their needs in the political realm. Even liberals who would normally champion their cause are largely silent. And in the workplace, they are without unions or associations to represent their interests.

Still, the rules of the game governing work and its rewards are up to us. It is our values that we bring to these choices. Whether we give basic rights to these workers and give them more power to change their conditions is our choice. Whether we ensure that workers have "family-supporting" wages and benefits says a great deal about what kind of society and com-

munities we want to live in. So far we have given these workers
few tools to improve their lives. In fact, in most cases, we have
blocked the road to change.

Without change, a growing gap between the haves and have-
nots will continue to challenge our national solidarity and stability and will strain an already divisive America. But just as
important, if work does not work for millions of Americans it
undermines our country's most fundamental ideals. We are per-
mitting a caste system to grow up around us, consigning millions of Americans to a social dead-end. The notion of equal
opportunity becomes a farce in the face of these harsh class divi-
sions. It is a sentence passed onto not only those now toiling in
the poverty wage economy, but onto many of their children who
lack the support they need to succeed.

On a practical level, the quality of our services depends on
improving these workers' conditions. One of the things we
learned after the murderous attacks of September 11 is that
we had left the safety of the skies in the hands of the marketplace. Policy makers allowed individual airlines to watch after
our security at the airport gates. These corporations opted for the
cheapest solution and outsourced the work to private contractors. Winning contractors made the lowest bids by providing
their employees with some of the most miserably paid, poorly
benefited jobs in the United States, which led to high turnover
and untrained workers. They won the contracts, and the American people lost their security.

As a result of the terrorist assault, there was a move to improve airport security by bettering the wages and working conditions for the women and men who would staff these jobs. This

is a lesson we can apply much more broadly. Home health-care aides and child-care workers, janitors and hotel workers may not provide the immediacy of airline safety, but they do supply our most essential needs. And quality of service naturally suffers when workers feel cheated and demeaned. Do we really want an angry, resentful, and untrained workforce handling the chicken we eat, cleaning our hotels and offices, let alone taking care of our children or our parents?

If we honor work, we must reward it. For generations, Americans shared a tacit understanding that if you worked hard, a livable income and basic securities were to be yours. That promise has been broken and as a nation we are living a lie.

Some maintain that it would take too much effort and too much money to make these "bad" jobs into "good" ones. But incremental improvements make fundamental changes in workers' lives—a family-supporting wage, affordable health insurance, an ability to have a few days off for sickness or family needs, predictability in a work schedule, and more control over one's life. These changes can be the difference between workers seeing a future and seeing only despair.

This book offers ways to level the playing field for employers who are "doing the right thing" in providing their workers with livable wages, basic benefits, and respect. It presents an agenda that helps block the low road of degradation and moves to rebalance the power between employers and their workers. It proposes a Compact with Working Americans that will ensure the basics of a decent life for all working Americans and their families. This is not a radical proposal. In the past, we have established standards and rights to ensure that older Americans would not be impoverished or go without health care, to prevent children from working, to keep our environment clean, and to guarantee that workers have equal opportunity regardless of their race, religion, national origin, sex, or age. Now we must do so to protect the well-being of all working families and the moral integrity of the nation.

CHAPTER 1

Three Workers

LINDA STEVENS (FLINT, MICHIGAN)

Linda Stevens wants to put aside money for her daughter Sharon's college education. Since Sharon first held a basketball, she has loved the sport and hopes to qualify for a college basketball scholarship. A solid B student, even at twelve years old she has her eyes set on the University of Tennessee. The hope of sending Sharon to college is what keeps Linda going, but so far she has been unable to afford to save.

When I first met Linda five years ago, she was working at Kessell Food Store, a small grocery store chain in Flint, Michigan. She prepared and served meals in the store's food court. After two and a half years, she made $5.25 an hour. As a part-timer, working twenty-five hours a week, she received no vacation and no paid sick leave from her employer. While Medicaid covered her daughter, she herself had no health insurance. When she slipped and hurt her hip, she ran up a $1,000 medical bill she is still paying off.

Linda hates to be in debt. That attitude is born of a solid working-class African-American background. A tall, striking woman with a clear sense of purpose, she took college preparatory courses during her high school years in Flint. After graduating, she took courses at the local junior college. But marriage interrupted her studies and she didn't get a degree. Her dream was to be a business lawyer. She stayed at home and raised her four children, three older boys who are now grown and working, and Sharon. In 1994, she and her husband, Robert, separated and divorced after fifteen years of marriage. The first two years, he paid child support and alimony, but in 1996 he injured his arm at his construction job and could no longer work. While he receives workmen's compensation, it barely supports him. So at forty-two, Linda had to become the principal breadwinner for her family.

The only job she could find with a high school degree and some college courses was a part-time cashier's position at a small market called George and Stanley's, working the night shift from 6:00 P.M. to 10:00 P.M. Not surprisingly, the $5.00 an hour she made at her retail job was not enough to support her and her daughter, so she worked a second job from 2:00 to 5:00 P.M. as a receptionist at H&R Block, which paid $5.50 an hour. She liked the work and would have preferred to go full-time, but H&R Block only offered work from January through April. The money from these two part-time jobs still did not cover her bills, so she worked as a lunch supervisor for the Flint public schools from 11:30 A.M. to 1:00 P.M. She had to put planners up on the wall to keep track of her schedule. And even then, she had no benefits.

After a year, Linda left her job at George and Stanley's after they refused to give her a 25 cent raise and went to work at Kessell's on the day shift for $5.25 an hour. But Kessell (which has since been purchased by Kroger) would only give her a part-time position and without full-time status, she still did not get benefits. Working three jobs became so exhausting that she left her lunch supervisor position, but had to continue to work her second job at H&R Block.

Linda's typical day started at 6:00 A.M. when she got her daughter ready for school. Her job at Kessell started at 7:00 A.M. and ended at 3:00 P.M. She came home, changed, and went to her job at H&R Block at 5:00 P.M. and got off at 10:00 P.M. Her schedule left little time to spend with her daughter.

Three years ago, Kessell told Linda that she could have a full-time job. She thought it was a step toward her dreams. At least with a full-time job she thought she could see a future. She could plan. She could put some money away for her daughter's education. With the full-time position, she could move to a safer neighborhood. But she admits, "Now that I'm full-time, it's not all that I expected."

Kessell switched her job from food court clerk to bakery clerk. She got a $1.00 increase to $6.25. "The good part of full-time status is that I qualify for the company's health insurance," she says (it costs her $68.00 a month). But Linda still makes so little that she must continue to work at her second job at H & R Block.

And as she points out, "No one understands what gives you full-time status or the reasons for getting it. Only five percent of the employees get categorized as full-time. I really want to get out of my neighborhood to a safe place for my daughter. But I can't move because of all the uncertainty. I need to know whether this change is going to be permanent."

Linda lives in what she describes as a "rough neighborhood." "There's gambling, drinking and drugs in the neighborhood. Kids hang out on the street. The neighborhood kids don't respect their parents." Linda won't let her daughter go out when she's not there.

She wants to move, but she can't afford it. Even working full-time, it's hard to pay the bills. With subsidized housing, her rent went up to $350, and she is trying to hang on to her phone. Last winter, she came home and her water had been cut off because she couldn't pay her bill. The Salvation Army finally helped get it turned back on.

After six years as a breadwinner, Linda admits she's discouraged. "I work hard. I take care of my customers. But I feel like I'm being stabbed in the back. The owner keeps telling me that we are family. But this is no way to treat family. Sometimes I want to give up but I know I can't. I have a child to raise. I want my daughter to think that if you are honest and do your best then the sky's the limit. I want my daughter to have a future, go to college, have the opportunities I didn't have. But it is hard when you can't save for her future. That is the hardest part."

FLOR SEGUNDA (NEWARK, NEW JERSEY)

What you first notice about Flor Segunda is her black shiny hair and her dark smiling eyes. She is a small woman with enormous energy and an activist fire, though she looks older than her thirty-five years. She and her husband, Manuel, came to this country from Ecuador with her brother ten years ago to find good jobs. In Ecuador, she graduated high school and took some accounting classes, but neither she nor Manuel could find work.

Flor lives in a primarily African-American neighborhood of Newark, New Jersey, with her husband and three children: Jose, who is nine years old; Luis, who is two and a half; and Paul, who is one and a half. To reach Flor's place, you must walk down a flight of concrete stairs, through a narrow hall, and past the washer and dryer. Like most basement apartments, it is damp and dark. One small window allows the only daylight to enter. They pay $700 per month for this two-bedroom apartment without utilities. There are no parks near her apartment and she doesn't have a car. So most days, the children stay inside.

Flor understands some English but has a hard time speaking the language, which makes it difficult to talk with her neighbors. She began English classes when she first came to this country, but one day, seven months pregnant and on her way home from class, a man pushed her against a fence and robbed her. Her husband did not want her to continue. Later on, "once I had my children, it was difficult to find the time and afford the classes and a baby-sitter. I still want to go back to school," Flor says. "I've always loved to go to school."

At night when most workers are at home, Flor begins her day. She cleans, dusts, vacuums, dumps trash, and straightens the offices of law firms in a large suburban office building in West Orange, New Jersey. Flor is a janitor. She works for a private contractor who contracts with the owners of commercial buildings to provide cleaning services. After eight years, she still makes

$6.00 an hour, although her wages are 50 cents higher than her coworkers' because she has more square feet of office space to clean. "We get nothing," she says, "no health insurance, paid vacation leave, or retirement plan." If she gets sick, she either loses a day's pay or works sick.

Her husband is a day laborer. He gets up to go stand on a corner by 6:00 A.M. in the hopes of getting picked up for odd construction jobs. His day ends around 6:00 P.M. He makes $9.00 an hour, but the work is not steady. If he works three days a week he considers himself lucky, and in the wintertime it is especially difficult. He gets no benefits of any kind. He only gets the wages he makes if he works that day. Because of a cerebral hemorrhage in 1994, he is only supposed to do light jobs. But he needs the work.

Their expenses add up. Besides their $700 rent, there is $200 for utilities, $40 for laundry, $40 for transportation and nearly $400 for food. They pay $100 a month to a fifteen-year-old teenager to cover the couple of hours in the evening when Flor has left for work and Manuel has not yet come home. Without health insurance, each child's visit to a doctor costs $50. Her husband must spend $76 per month for his medicines. Each time Flor had a child, they had to live only on Manuel's wages. Her employer provides no paid family leave. Money was so short one time that they had to move in with her brother.

In April 2001, Flor was out of work for a different reason. After she and five of her coworkers sent a letter to their boss asking for a pay increase, they were all fired. She was out of work for seven months and she only got her job back when a Service Employees International Union Local helped her file charges with the National Labor Relations Board for illegally discharging her. But being out of work for so long put her behind in her payments. She still owes $450 dollars in utility bills.

Flor continues to lead the fight to improve the janitorial jobs by trying to organize her Latino coworkers into a union. "I want a better life for myself and my children," she says. "Manuel supports me even though it's scary sometimes. I'm afraid I might get fired again. But it's the only way it will get better."

BOB BUTLER (ALBERTVILLE, ALABAMA)

"It's dangerous in there," says Bob. Bob Butler works at a poultry plant in rural Albertville, Alabama. He has worked there for over eight years on the 2:00 P.M. to 10:30 P.M. shift. He gets premium pay for sharpening the knives and scissors that the plant workers use to slice and cut the chickens as they move through the line. His $8.20-an-hour pay is the highest wage in the plant because it is reserved for those who are considered the most skilled. Bob loves sharpening knives. But he rankles at where he must do it. "I'm working in a hog pen, sharpening knives to use on fresh meat to sell on the street," he says. Bob's area is covered with grinding powder. When it rains, water drips through the roof onto the electric machines. He has fourteen stitches in his finger from a recent injury. "The plant supervisor told me to keep working," he recalls, but he didn't want to get blood all over the knives.

Bob is a big, tough-talking man with tattoos running down his neck. He is one of the only whites in a plant that is largely Latino. He takes a lot of pride in his work, and complains that management is "forcing me to put out a substandard product because of the speed they want me to sharpen the knives. The company puts the line speed so fast that it's hurting people. They give them bad knives." He's the only person sharpening knives for two hundred workers. "And if the knives are not sharp, workers hurt their hands. Their hands get numb. They are killing people in there. And you don't have any sick days. You just have to keep working."

He bristles when he talks about how the company treats the workers. "They treat people like animals. If you have to go to the bathroom, they write you up for being away from the line for what they say is an excessive period of time. You only have a certain amount of chits a week for going to the bathroom. If you use more than that, they fire you. If you take more than five minutes, you will get disciplined. Five minutes isn't enough time to get your uniform off, go to the bathroom, wait for a stall, and get back to the line. If there is no one to replace you, they won't let you go. We've had people do it on the line and then walk off and go home.

"The company doesn't care about the people. Nothing gets done by the company to stop injuries. There was a small guy pushing a big cart; biggest thing on this guy was his boots. He was pushing this cart and it fell over because it hit an open drain. The supervisor took him in the office and wrote him up. They never fixed the open drain. This guy's pushing this stuff as fast as he can, he's killing himself and he's supposed to see the hole in the floor. The only way you get something done is if a person is sucked up in a machine or their hand is cut off. Then they'll get written up for getting hurt.

"If they took care of the people there would be less turnover. There would be less injuries. They care more about the chickens than us. But we have families like everyone else." Bob supports his mother and his sister. After high school, he moved from Albertville up north to find a good job. A Teamster, he made a good living working in a distribution center. He married but was divorced after several years. When his elderly mother became ill in 1991, and with no children of his own to support, he moved back to Albertville to take care of her and his sister. His choice of work was limited to farming, owning his own business, or working in the poultry processing plants. "One processing plant is no different than working in another," Bob says. "It's the sorriest mess I've ever seen. You'd be surprised what that one little piece of chicken you're going to eat this Sunday has cost these people."

CHAPTER 2

Piling On: Why It's About More Than Money

Working in a low-wage job in the United States means you are paid a wage insufficient to meet your families' basic needs. But inadequate wages are only the beginning. Low-wage jobs also mean few or no benefits, rigid schedules, late-night shifts, unsafe and unhealthy conditions, and lack of respect.[1] It is this "piling on" that makes low-wage jobs not just quantitatively different than better paying jobs, but qualitatively different. These are the things that make low-wage work a world apart.

WHAT'S A LOW WAGE: WHAT IT TAKES TO MAKE ENDS MEET

Even during the best of economic times in the late nineties, one out of every four workers earned less than $8.70 per hour.* For

---

*Any definition of a low-wage job is somewhat arbitrary. Where do you draw the line? This book focuses on jobs that pay between $5 and $9 per hour, but also have a myriad of other deficits that higher paying jobs do not have. $8.70 is the hourly wage for a 40-hour workweek for a family of four that is at the government-defined poverty level.

these thirty million Americans, this amounts to an annual income of $18,100 if they were working full-time, the government-defined poverty level for a family of four.[2] Wages rose in the late nineties, due primarily to the tightest labor market since 1969, but overall pay for low-end jobs has declined over the past twenty years.[3] And not surprisingly, in the economic turndown, these small gains were the first to go.[4]

America's bottom-end workers fare worse than their counterparts in other industrialized countries.[5] Comparable German workers earn more than twice as much.[6] While the bottom 10 percent of American workers earn just 37 percent of the U.S. median wage, similar workers in other industrialized countries earn 60–76 percent of their country's median wage.[7] And America's low-wage workers also have lower standards of living. Other industrialized countries provide health care, child care, and education to their citizenry—Americans must pay for these services out of pocket.[8]

What does it mean to earn enough to support oneself and one's family? Policy makers since the sixties have looked to the official poverty rate as the standard for measuring an adequate income. In 2002, the official poverty threshold for a family of four (two adults and two children) was an annual household income of $18,100.[9] But that standard erroneously assumes that food constitutes one-third of a family's budget and merely multiplies that amount by three in reaching the "official" poverty rate. Today, however, housing, health care, and work expenses such as child care and transportation are some of a family's largest expenditures, and food constitutes less than 20 percent of a household's budget.[10] Most leading scholars agree that this measure is wholly inadequate and outdated.[11] In a recent survey of Americans, most concluded that the official poverty rate grossly underestimates what it takes to make ends meet.[12]

Some state governments have caught on to this fact and regularly bypass the official poverty rate. To qualify for the Children's Health Insurance Program (CHIP), for example, many states use 150–200 percent of the official poverty level to determine eligibility, and a few states go as high as 275–300 percent. Medicaid expansions and the food stamp program also use figures above the poverty level to determine eligibility.

So how much do people need to make ends meet? There is no perfect measure for determining the amount needed to provide for family self-sufficiency. In a recent study by the Economic Policy Institute, researchers looked at family budgets and how much it would cost in various geographic areas to provide basic housing, health care, food, child care, transportation, and other essentials. They concluded that in many places it took more than double the official poverty rate to provide for a family's basic needs.[13]

To be sure, not all low-wage workers are in low-income families. Some low-wage workers are lucky enough to have other adults in their families who make more. This does not obviate the inadequacy of the wage they are paid, or the myriad of other hardships of their jobs. It does, however, allow them to have a decent standard of living. But most low-wage workers are in families like those of Linda Stevens, Bob Butler, Cynthia Porter, and Flor Segunda and can't make ends meet.[14]

What does it mean on a practical level to earn too little? It means being in constant peril of eviction.[15] Families with incomes twice the official poverty rate are more than twice as likely to miss rent payments or be evicted.[16] Even working two jobs, Linda Stevens, the retail worker from Flint, owes back rent. She had to go to court to hold on to her apartment. But now she has to pay a late charge, squeezing the money left to pay her utilities.

Earning too little means sharing housing with others or renting rooms in motels. A recent study concluded that an average worker would have to earn at least $13.87 an hour to be able to afford the rent of a two-bedroom apartment and $14.66 to rent a two-bedroom home.[17] This is nearly three times the federal minimum wage. Unable to afford stable housing, low-wage families move more often—three times in the last five years for Flor, the Newark janitor—constantly disrupting their families' lives.[18]

Having a low income means being four times more likely than the nonpoor to have your utilities cut off.[19] In arrears for $150, Cynthia Porter, the nursing home aide from Marian, recently lost her heat and electricity. "I will have to get a kerosene lamp," she says. "I have a child with asthma and when it gets cold, he gets sick, so I need heat." Like Cynthia, many low-wage workers have no phone. If they do, they are five times as likely to have it cut off.[20] Credit is harder to obtain, so many rent furniture and appliances that cost far more than purchasing them.

Having an inadequate income means skipping meals.[21] It means living in neighborhoods with higher incidents of crime and being more likely to be the victim of a crime. In Flor Segunda's new neighborhood, there are drug deals on a regular basis. She's been assaulted and robbed.

Having limited resources makes it difficult to get to work. One in three low-wage workers do not have a car and in many cities bus and subway services stop running at night or don't reach poor neighborhoods. For many, taking or losing a job comes down to whether a ride is available.

Different people face different hardships, of course, but some problems are common to low-wage work. And those problems affect some of the core areas of life: health, stability, family, safety, respect, and security.

HEALTH: WHY LOW-WAGE WORKERS CAN'T GET SICK

More than any other industrialized country, we have relied on the private sector to supply health coverage.[22] One hundred and fifty-eight million Americans obtain employer-provided health coverage either as an employee or as a spouse or child of an employee.[23] Yet more than forty million Americans have no health insurance, an increase of about ten million from 1988. Eight out of ten are in working families, and over half of the uninsured Americans and—strikingly—two-thirds of uninsured children live in families headed by workers with incomes below 200 percent of the poverty line.[24]

Most low-wage jobs do not provide health insurance. In 1995, less than half the workers making under $20,000 a year ($10.00 an hour working full-time) were offered health insurance by their employer, in contrast to over 80 percent of workers making over $40,000 a year.[25] Many low-wage jobs are in smaller firms and an alarming two-thirds of small employers fail to offer low-wage workers health insurance.[26] Some workers receive coverage from their spouse, but low-wage workers are less likely to have this option. That leaves one in four workers making less than $20,000 a year without insurance from any source.[27]

And many who are lucky enough to have an employer plan cannot afford it.[28] At Cynthia Porter's nursing home, employees must pay $80 a month ($960 per year) for individual coverage and $220 a month for family coverage ($2,640 per year). Costs are similar to those of firms with less than 200 workers, which are the vast majority of low-wage workplaces.[29] For Cynthia, who makes around $15,000 per year, this is well beyond her reach. Not surprisingly, the number of workers who have declined coverage from their employer has increased from 12 to 20 percent in the last ten years.[30] And the share of health-care contributions and deductibles paid by the employees continues to rise.[31]

The prospect for future coverage does not look bright.[32] The manufacturing sector, the area with the most health-care coverage, is in decline, while the low-wage service sectors that have among the lowest health-care coverage rates are anticipated to grow in the next decade.[33]

And what happens when workers and their families have no health coverage? Flor Segunda says that "doctors require immediate payment before they will see you, but many times I don't have the money. Right now, Luis has a temperature. But I try to take care of it myself because I can't afford to take him to the doctor every time. It is one of the reasons I don't like my children to play outside. They will get sick and I can't afford it."

Like Flor's, families without health insurance do not get routine and preventative examinations.[34] Instead, they rely on emergency rooms for their primary care. But emergency-room care is expensive. Linda Stevens's last visit cost $1,000. She is still trying to pay it off.

The workers who have the least employer-provided health insurance and the poorest health are also those with the least employer-sponsored sick pay. When Linda got tendonitis decorating hundreds of cakes during the Christmas season at her store, her employer's doctor said she could not work, but her employer refused to pay her while she recuperated. "I had to come back against the doctor's orders. I needed the money." Like Linda, more than 60 percent of low-wage workers are not paid when they are out sick.[35]

Losing pay is only one of the problems faced by low-wage workers when they get sick or injured. "Anytime you are off work you get an 'occurrence,' " Dennis Simpson, a call-center worker from Arlington, Texas, explains. "If you are off sick, an emergency, your child is sick, it doesn't matter, you get an 'occurrence.' If you get three, they put you on probation. You can lose your job. There is no slack. There are no excuses. It doesn't matter whether you are only off for a day at a time. Three occurrences and you are disciplined."

FEWER HOURS AND MORE EVENING SHIFTS: WHY LOW-WAGE WORKERS CAN'T GET A STEADY DAY JOB

Low-wage jobs provide fewer and more unpredictable hours than higher paid positions.[36] A majority of the twenty-one million part-time jobs are low-wage.[37] These jobs are concentrated in low-wage industries with the wholesale and retail trades and services alone employing close to 40 percent of the part-time workforce.[38] But describing these jobs as "part-time" makes them seem peripheral or unimportant. This is an artificial distinction. Some employers, especially in retail and services, have almost their entire workforce made up of people working less than forty hours a week. Many use a part-time workforce to give them more flexibility in scheduling. Still others simply do so to reduce their personnel expenses by not extending benefits to this part of the workforce.[39] These permanent part-time workers are the backbone of the employer's workforce.

Yet the average part-time worker gets paid 60 percent of the average wage rate of the full-time worker.[40] One quarter of part-time workers earn minimum wage, as compared to 5 percent of full-time workers.[41] Even in comparable jobs, part-time work pays on average 20 percent less.[42]

There are other disadvantages to regular "part-time" work. These workers have less chance of receiving health benefits, vacation, sick pay, pension, and family leave than full-time workers.[43] Only 13 percent of female part-timers and 20 percent of male part-timers have employer-provided health-care coverage.[44] Linda and Cynthia were excluded from participating in their employer's health plan, even though both were working over twenty-five hours per week. And in a cruel irony, the limited hours of numerous part-timers disqualifies them from many government-supported programs.

Low-wage jobs use more temporary workers than higher paid positions.[45] Of the 2.4 million workers employed by temporary help firms in 1996, six out of ten did work on the lowest end of the corporate job ladder.[46] These workers earn even less than full-time or part-time workers in similar jobs and less than one in ten agency temps are offered health insurance, while sick leave, family leave, and vacations are virtually nonexistent.[47] Only 21 percent are offered a pension plan and only 7 percent can afford it.[48]

Yet it is these temporary workers who have the least protection under federal labor laws. Because many are not considered "employees," they are exempted from many of the protections of labor statutes such as the National Labor Relations Act and the Fair Labor Standards Act. Still others are not covered by unemployment compensation laws or the Family and Medical Leave Act.

Even for full-time workers, the number of hours are less predictable than those in higher paid positions. Darlene Stewart is technically classified as full-time at the Reno hotel where she works. But without notice, her employer cuts back her hours when occupancy is low. The winter months are the worst. In January, February, and March they cut her schedule from five days to two. "It's impossible to predict how many hours you are going to work. So you can't get another job. It's really hard to make it through. You never know when you are going to get 'early out.' "

Approximately one-third of Americans work night shifts, but while twenty years ago these shifts were fairly evenly distributed amongst high- and low-wage workers, today that has changed.[49] More than 75 percent of the cashiers, food prep workers, nursing aides, orderlies and attendants, retail sales, and waitresses work nonstandard hours.[50] Now it is workers with the fewest resources that confront the difficulties of these schedules—added health risks, exposure to violence and accidents, and more expensive and less available child care.[51]

FAMILY: WHY LOW-WAGE WORKERS CAN'T WORK AND PROPERLY CARE FOR THEIR CHILDREN

Most Americans juggle work and family life. But for low-wage workers it is more than an issue of juggling. In many cases, it requires sacrificing the needs of one's family to have a job.

The lack of sick leave and family leave in low-wage jobs makes a child's simple cold or an emergency at school a potential disaster. In the rare instance that these workers are offered sick leave, most companies refuse to allow workers to use that time for a sick child.[52] For those workers who can take a day off for a child's illness, most won't get paid. While close to half of all workers with young children are able to take paid time off for their sick child, only one-third of low-wage parents enjoy the same privilege.[53]

The Family and Medical Leave Act (FMLA) does little to redress this situation. While it allows leave for a serious illness, it does not provide leave for the day-to-day illnesses that most families face. Moreover, it excludes part-timers and fails to cover employers with fifty or fewer workers, disqualifying a majority of low-end employers. But even if a low-wage worker is covered under the Act, it provides only for unpaid leave.

And it's not just illnesses, as Linda Stevens observes. "I don't get time for PTA or anything else with my child. If I take time, they won't make time up during the week so you lose a day's pay." Fewer than one out of ten workers in a low-wage job have any employer-provided family leave.[54] And if these workers can get time off, they won't be paid.

Of course, it is these workers who are also provided few if any vacation days.[55] Eighty percent of full-time American workers receive paid holidays and vacations, but less than 10 percent of the workers in the bottom tenth of wage-earners receive these benefits.[56] For low-wage parents with children under six, one-third don't have access to paid vacations or paid holidays.[57]

And low-wage jobs have the most rigid schedules. Twenty-six percent of working parents have access to daily flextime, but only 13 percent of low-wage parents can adjust their start and finish time daily.[58] And low-wage workplaces often penalize workers for being a few minutes late. A five-minute delay because of a sick child, late baby-sitter, or missed bus can lead to discipline, a dock in pay, or discharge.

"And they don't take your situation into consideration when they schedule you," Linda explains. "They told me they might ship me out to different stores. But I have to pick my daughter up after school and take her home, and if the store is far away, I can't do that. If you don't go where they want, you lose your job."

Mandatory overtime further complicates matters. The "dot" system is a good example. When an employee is absent at Cynthia Porter's nursing home, the supervisor merely puts a dot next to a worker's name to indicate that he or she must fill in for the absent worker on the next shift. "That's really hard," Cynthia says. "Most of us have children. We have to pick them up or they expect us at home. But the company doesn't care what your circumstances are. They just put a dot next to your name. That's that."

And these workers do not have the luxury of taking time off from work after their children are born. The FMLA only guarantees people twelve weeks of unpaid job-protected leave to care for a new baby, and those who work less than 1,250 hours during the previous twelve months don't even qualify for coverage under the Act.[59]

The average annual cost for child care is $5,000, close to one-fourth of many low-wage workers' incomes.[60] Families earning $50,000 or more, in contrast, pay only 6 percent of their earnings for child care.[61] Without the ability to afford quality child care or adult supervision for their children, many low-wage women are forced to work fewer hours, which reduces their already meager earnings.[62] This limitation is especially true for single mothers. The wages of many single mothers are so low that many must reduce their hours of paid work to the times when they can arrange for free child care from a friend or relative.[63] Still others are forced to patch together unpaid care of poorer quality.[64]

Many husbands and wives, like Flor and Manuel, work split shifts, one working days and the other evening or nights, to minimize child care expenses. "By the time Manuel comes home from work, I have left for work. When I get home around 11:30 P.M., Manuel is asleep. The next morning at 5:00 A.M. when Manuel leaves for work, I am asleep. It doesn't give us much time together. We only see each other and have family time on weekends." One-third of dual-earner couples with pre—school-aged children work these split shifts, creating pressures that fuel high divorce levels that are three to six times the national rate.[65] Still others work multiple jobs to make ends meet. Between 1973 and 1999, the proportion of employees working more than one job jumped from 5.1 to 6.3 percent, with nearly eight million workers holding multiple jobs in 1999.[66]

Late-night shifts make obtaining child care even more difficult.[67] Every time Linda's employer schedules her to work evenings, she faces a dilemma. She only gets a few days' notice. So Sharon, her twelve-year old daughter, often stays home alone. "I'm scared for her every moment I'm at work," she says.

SAFETY: WHY LOW-WAGE JOBS ARE UNSAFE

While higher wage jobs have become safer over the past twenty years, low-wage jobs have become increasingly more dangerous.[68] Today, cashiers, nursing home workers, food processing workers, janitors, security guards, waitresses, child care workers, and other low-wage workers work under more hazardous conditions.

The poultry processing industry is one of the most dangerous industries. Poultry processing workers repeat the same slice or cut on chickens as many as 40,000 times a day. They do these cuts on chickens speeding down a line at an average rate of ninety-one birds per minute or a bird and a half per second.[69] These repetitive motions, performed eight hours a day in cold temperatures, permanently damage these workers' hands, shoulders, and wrists. Nearly one in five poultry processing workers suffered a serious injury in 1995, double the injury rate of a decade before and twice the rate of other manufacturing injuries.[70] The number of injuries could be reduced if companies would slow down the lines and rotate workers among different jobs. Instead, companies doubled the line speeds over the past fifteen years and do little to rotate workers.[71]

Mary Thomas walks with a limp from her injuries at a Kentucky chicken processing plant where she works. Chicken fat is everywhere in the plant, but the bathroom tile is especially slippery. The workers repeatedly complained to the manager about the floor, but five years went by before the employer did anything about it. During that time, Mary fell three times, injuring her leg and shoulder.

Retail jobs like Linda's cause other health problems for workers. Repetitive motion injuries, such as carpal tunnel syndrome and tendonitis, back sprains, and muscle strains are the most common difficulties retail workers face. The grocery store industry ranks third in total recordable injuries and illnesses.[72] And workplace violence, most prevalent in retail, is the second leading cause of job-related deaths for all workers and the number-one cause for women.[73]

Earl Craig, Linda's coworker, is on his knees for eight hours straight, starting at 11 P.M., waxing and cleaning the floors of a 50,000-square-foot supermarket. He has a burning sensation under his knees, and his shoulders and arms ache constantly. He has had to work nineteen days straight without a break because his employer hasn't trained anyone else to do the job. He can't ask for time off because he fears they will fire him. It's hard at forty-six years of age.

Nursing aides, home health-care workers and orderlies suffer more injuries and illnesses to their backs than all construction trades put together.[74] This makes sense. Nurse's aides' and home health-care aides' jobs require constant lifting. Cynthia works the night shift that is always short-staffed. Many nights, there are only two certified nursing assistants for forty-three residents, leaving her alone to lift, turn, and walk residents who can weigh more than two hundred pounds. Many of the residents are Alzheimer patients who sometimes resist her. Three years ago, Cynthia hurt her back lifting a resident.

Call-center workers suffer from depression, extreme anxiety, headaches, back pain, shoulder soreness, and stiff or sore wrists.[75] "In my office of thirty-eight reps, five are out on stress-related disability," explains Patricia Stanton, a Texas call-center operator. "Three more have colitis and another has an ulcer. We have big boxes of Motrin that we share. Not a day goes by that I don't take a Motrin for headaches."

Patricia's office is not unique. Stress-related illnesses and injuries plague the call-center industry. Nonstop telephone time with customers—many of whom can be difficult and insulting, strict production requirements, and pervasive employer surveillance are responsible for this plague of physical and nervous disorders. "It's as close to a sweatshop as you can get," says Dennis Simpson. "The management keeps pressuring you for more and more production. Once you sign on your shift, you can't sign off."

Failure to stick to the schedule is considered a "deviation" and punishable by disciplinary action. "Deviations" may include such things as staying on the line too long with a customer, closing your phone to incoming calls to call another department to solve a problem or to do a few minutes of paperwork, or taking too long to log into the system. Punishment is likely if a worker goes to the bathroom or gets a drink of water off schedule or takes a sick day or an excused personal-leave day after the schedule has been issued.

Workers are constantly watched and monitored. Pressure builds and then boils over. Employee stress was the key issue in a 2000 Verizon call-center strike, where they were reprimanded for staying too long in the bathroom, disciplined for being thirty seconds late to work or after breaks, and denied vacation time.[76]

Back injuries and other muscle pulls and strains are a constant problem in the hotel and restaurant industries. Vevia Ross, a hotel utility porter, likes "shampooing the carpets and making the rooms really nice. But the heavy machines are hard to push and I have to get down on my hands and knees to scrub the carpet. I have bursitis from being on my knees doing the shampooing. But my boss doesn't care."

To be sure, many of the injuries in these low-wage jobs could be avoided. But like Linda's employer, who refused to supply mats for the slippery kitchen floors because he was afraid that the mats would slow the workers down, most do little to prevent accidents. And when workers do get injured, many low-wage employers do little to accommodate their needs. When Linda was working her first job at the store, preparing meals, she slipped and fell. The company doctor prescribed medication and therapy and light duty on the job. When she took the doctor's slip to her supervisor, he refused to give her light duty. They told her if she sat down she had to clock out. She couldn't work for one week. She lost six days of pay. Against the doctor's orders, she had to return to work hurt while still recovering from her injuries. Still other employers simply fire workers when they get injured.[77] And few workers are provided long-term disability insurance.[78]

DIGNITY: HOW LOW-WAGE WORKERS GET NO RESPECT

"You tell the supervisors that a resident in the nursing home isn't breathing right and they don't do anything," Cynthia explains. "They have a suggestion box. But they never take your advice. I have suggestions regarding the residents because I'm with them all the time, but they never listen."

Many low-wage workers face nothing less than outright contempt from their employers. "They think that they are in control of everything," says Barbara Barry, a casino worker. "They portray themselves as mighty rulers. They can fire you if they don't like how you comb your hair."

Some workplaces are even abusive. "My boss kept getting on

me real hard," Bill Jones, a packinghouse worker from Kentucky describes. "He would cuss me out all the time. He grabbed me by the arm. Every day he swore at me."

But it is the employers' daily treatment of low-wage workers as basically untrustworthy that is continually degrading. Unlike higher paying jobs in which workers are assumed to be acting in the interests of the company, lower-wage workers are assumed otherwise. To keep them in line, they are monitored, drug-tested, timed, and threatened with discipline.

Of course, bosses who demean their employees in this way are not apt to offer them much in the way of training and education. Those who receive training earn up to 16 percent in higher wages than comparable workers who lack such training.[79] Yet workers in low-wage jobs are half as likely to receive employer-sponsored education as workers in higher-wage jobs.[80] Cynthia would like to go back to school to be a licensed practical nurse. "I could earn at least two dollars to three dollars more per hour," she points out. But without support, Cynthia can't afford to go.

SECURITY: WHY LOW-WAGE WORKERS DON'T THINK ABOUT THE FUTURE

Not surprisingly, workers in low-wage jobs suffer more frequent and recurrent periods of unemployment.[81] And in an economic downturn, they are generally the first to go.[82] They do so with the least savings and support, and the fewest government benefits to cushion the blow. Few low-wage workers receive any severance pay.[83] Without support, they are unable to continue their health insurance should they be lucky enough to have any. Under

COBRA, workers have the right to continue coverage under their employers' health insurance plan for eighteen months. But workers must pay for the full amount of that coverage.

Once unemployed, these workers are the least apt to qualify for unemployment compensation insurance. Many requirements of the federal/state unemployment compensation laws discriminate on the basis of income.[84] In most states, there are minimum earnings and workweek requirements for eligibility. These exclude many low-wage workers, especially part-timers, and require them to work more hours than higher-paid workers to qualify. Many low-wage workers leave work because they are unable to find adequate child care or transportation to work, reasons that generally do not qualify for coverage under most unemployment laws. And to receive unemployment benefits, a worker must be willing to work full-time, an impossibility for many low-wage women with small children.[85]

At the end of their careers, low-wage workers will have little to look forward to. Their jobs provide few retirement benefits. Eighty-four percent of the workers with annual earnings of $50,000 or more are offered a retirement plan by their employers, and 90 percent of those workers participate.[86] For workers making between $10,000 and $15,000 a year, less than half were offered an employer-provided plan.[87]

For those low-wage workers lucky enough to be offered a retirement plan, many cannot afford it.[88] As Linda Stevens explains, "There is really no employer-paid pension. There is something you can pay into, but I can't afford it. I need all the money I can to take care of my daughter." In the end, less than one in five workers with incomes below $20,000 have pension coverage—workers with the fewest assets and the least savings.[89] With little or no savings and no employer-provided pensions, low-wage workers face a grim conclusion to their working lives.

·   ·   ·

If we are to address work not working for these Americans, we must examine their jobs. When we begin to do so, we will find low-wage workers occupying positions of importance in nearly all aspects of our lives—at home, at work, and when we travel.

CHAPTER 3

In the Heart of Our Economy and Our Lives

Low-wage jobs and the workers in these jobs are intimately involved in every aspect of American life. The country's recent prosperity rests on the growing sectors of the economy in which they work. Yet in spite of their contributions, these jobs and the workers in these jobs are dismissed and undervalued. It is the part of our economy that remains invisible. It is time to take a closer look at these jobs and the many roles they play in all of our lives.

Contrary to the dominant myth that most low-wage jobs are the ones you see in your neighborhood McDonald's, fast-food jobs constitute less than 5 percent of all low-end jobs.[1] Then where do we find the people working in these low-wage, low-reward jobs? They are all around us: security guards, nurse's aides and home health-care aides, child-care workers and educational assistants, maids and porters, 1-800 call-center workers, bank tellers, data-entry keyers, cooks, food-preparation workers, waiters and waitresses, cashiers and pharmacy assistants, hairdressers and manicurists, parking-lot attendants, hotel receptionists and clerks, ambulance drivers, poultry, fish, and meat processors, sewing-machine operators, laundry and dry-cleaning operators, and agricultural workers.

These jobs require knowledge, patience, care, and communication skills. Most of them require constant interaction with people, whether they are a patient in a health-care setting, a child in a day-care center, a guest in a hotel, a tenant in a commercial office building, or a customer in a department store.[2] Yet, jobs requiring these human-relational skills continue to be viewed as less important than mechanical or technical skills that require little human contact.

As important as these jobs are, most of us do not even notice them. When we do so, it is almost always in a negative light. Low-wage jobs are lumped together and referred to as "hamburger flippers." This label insinuates a lack both of real skill and of social value. Even policy analysts and public officials refer to these jobs by the phrase "low-wage, low-skilled," as if the two terms were inseparable. This label mistakenly assumes that if a job pays poorly, it must be because it does not call for many skills. Many also erroneously equate the absence of a college education with the absence of job skills. These misguided assumptions preclude us from seeing the real demands and skills of these jobs. But first we need to see how these jobs fit into our overall economy.

LOW-WAGE JOBS IN THE SERVICE ECONOMY

Low-wage jobs are principally found in the service sector. This is no coincidence. In the last half of the twentieth century, the United States became a service economy rather than a manufacturing one. Wal-Mart is the largest creator of jobs. Less than forty years ago, one out of every three nonfarm jobs was in the manufacturing sector.[3] As recently as the seventies, it provided jobs to almost one-third of men between the ages of twenty-five and fifty-four who did not attend college. Entering the twenty-first century, however, manufacturing comprises only 16 percent of the total economy, or one out of every six jobs. By the year 2008, it is estimated that it will comprise only 12 percent of the total U.S. labor force.[4]

As manufacturing has shrunk, so has the number of middle-income jobs.[5] In 1983, these middle-income jobs constituted 44 percent of the workforce. It is projected that number will decline to 39 percent by 2005.[6] Many of these middle-income jobs were in large-scale manufacturing, which provided workers an average yearly income of $34,500.[7] This was especially true for jobs traditionally held by men.[8]

Meanwhile, the service-producing sector has dramatically expanded. In 1947, service-sector industries accounted for only half of all hours of employment. A half-century later, approximately 80 percent of the 134 million nonfarm jobs are in the service producing industries: retail trade, transportation, telecommunications, utilities, wholesale trade, finance, insurance and real estate, federal, state, and local government, and services.[9] The broad *service* category is comprised of health services, social services, administrative support services, personal services, entertainment and recreation services, and business services.

The media trumpeted the "new economy" and its creation of millions of well-paid, "knowledge" jobs such as engineers, lawyers, social scientists, architects, professors, doctors, and writers, as well as a myriad of executive, administrative, and managerial occupations. High-end occupations, in fact, grew from 17 percent of the American workforce in 1950 to almost a third by 1995 and is expected to add another 7.7 million jobs in the next ten years.[10]

Beyond these well-paying occupations the service economy encompasses a middle sector of jobs in transportation, telecommunications and utilities, and public administration and education. The median wages in these industries are $12.50, $14.01, and over $20, respectively. This compares to $10 in the overall service sector and $11.47 in manufacturing.[11] Not coincidentally, these three industries are the most highly unionized sectors of the service economy.[12]

There is a third segment of the service economy that is the least publicized and least discussed. It is the low-wage sectors that account for nearly two-thirds of America's low-wage jobs and are concentrated in retail trade and health, social administrative support, personal, entertainment and recreation, and business services.[13]

These low-end service and retail jobs produce 30 percent of the United States gross domestic product and are in industries whose profits doubled between 1993 and 1998.[14] Yet their median wages are the lowest in the U.S. economy: $6.50 in retail trade and ranging from a high of $9.30 in business and repair services to a low of $6.50 in personal services.[15] A full-time worker at $6.50 an hour earns a gross annual salary of $13,570. Even at the high end, a full-time worker would make less than $20,000 per year. But the harsh reality is that more than one-third of retail trade jobs and one-fourth of service jobs are only part-time.[16] And working part-time, these same jobs provide an average annual income of only $6,962 in retail and $9,932 in services.[17]

It is important to note that there are also millions of low-end jobs outside of the service sector: seven million in manufacturing, principally in food processing, food packing, and food canning, textile and machine operations, and laborer occupations; and one million in agriculture, where workers are principally engaged in fruit and vegetable picking. These millions of low-paying jobs in services, manufacturing, and agriculture have one thing in common—the lowest unionization rates in the United States. Less than 6 percent of the jobs that pay below $8.70 per hour are organized as contrasted with a 22 percent unionization rate for jobs that pay more than $15 an hour.[18]

And what of the future? The service sector will not only remain the dominant source of employment in the first decade of the century, but it will also be the dominant source of economic output in the U.S. economy.[19] Through 2010, it is projected that virtually all twenty-two million new jobs will be in the non-manufacturing industries with retail trade and low-end services expected to account for the large majority.[20] Similarly, nearly 60 percent of the output growth in the service-producing sector is projected to take place in these service industries.[21]

Five of the ten occupations anticipated to have the largest real job growth between 2000 and 2010 are in the lowest pay occupations: food preparation and service workers, retail salespersons, cashiers, security guards, and waiters and waitresses. And of the next twenty occupations with the largest predicted job growth, more than half are in low-wage service jobs: janitors, home health aides, nursing aides, laborers, landscapers, teachers' assistants, receptionists and information clerks, child-care workers, packagers, medical assistants, and personal and home-care aides.[22] Put another way, jobs that require no education and training beyond high school except on-the-job training will account for 57 percent of the job growth between 2000 and 2010.[23] Only 27 percent of U.S. jobs will require a bachelor's degree or above.[24]

As important as these numbers are in describing the realities of the new economy, we need to move beyond a quantitative picture to a qualitative one. We need to closely examine what these low-wage jobs are really all about. Many of the old stereotypes mask their diversity, their difficulty, and their importance. We must look more closely at these jobs.

THE JOBS

1-800 CALL-CENTER WORKER

"Hello, this is Ellen speaking, can I help you?" Another afternoon begins. Ellen Nelson works in an Arlington, Texas, airline reservation center. When Ellen was hired, she received two months of training on how to cancel reservations, rearrange travel plans, figure out the cost of different travel arrangements, use frequent-flier miles, how to take an infant or a pet on the plane, and how to deal with passenger emergencies. She had to learn the city and country codes worldwide. There is little in print, so workers must know how to find all the information on the computer to respond to a customer's question.

Ellen works the 3:00 P.M. to 11:30 P.M. shift from Sunday through Thursday. But she arrives forty-five minutes before her shift to get ready. She takes any vacant cubicle and wipes off the computer and keyboard before she turns it on. She got sick a lot before she started cleaning the computer. "There are always a lot of changes," she says, "especially on Monday." It takes her fifteen minutes just to read all the new airline information and changes in schedules and prices. This is time for which she doesn't get paid.

She then becomes available to take calls on her shift. The calls are fed continuously into her phone, and her employer monitors the number and length of the calls and listens to her conversations with the customers. If she exceeds five minutes per call, she can be disciplined. The time constraint makes it difficult for Ellen when she talks with travel agents who have many clients or with customers who need instructions on how to buy tickets over the Internet. Her employer also records how much time she spends off the phone, called *slippage*. When Ellen takes time to finish paperwork or go to the bathroom, it is slippage that is docked against her. Too much can lead to discipline or being fired. In order to avoid being penalized, she doesn't take her two fifteen-minute breaks. "It is a lot of pressure and stress. There is no downtime," she says.

It's very noisy inside the call center. It is a twenty-four-hour a day, seven-day a week operation. Built on two levels, the center houses 2,600 agents over a twenty-four-hour period. From the entrance, you can see all the workstations. The agents are seated row after row for the entire length of the building. Ellen sits in a bay abutting other workers on either side and in front and in back of her. She hears other agents' phone conversations from all directions. Because the center is so large, it is impossible to regulate the temperature. You burn up in one workstation and freeze in another.

"It is hard to get to know anyone at work," Ellen laments. There are no real attachments in there. Without permanent workstations, there is generally someone new sitting next to you each time you come onto your shift. You don't have time to stop and visit anyway. During breaks and lunch, everyone is rushing to go to the bathroom and to the cafeteria, order food, eat it, and get back to their stations on time.

"Some of the customers are nice. That is the redeeming factor. But others are insulting to you. They yell at us because their flights are cancelled or they can't change a flight on a nonrefundable ticket. It is difficult because regardless of how a customer treats you, you have to be pleasant. That is your job. It's nonstop. I am a modern-day factory worker making a product that is a reservation."

· · ·

Ellen's job is one of the 3.3 million call-center jobs in the United States. With the advent of computerization, these jobs have become an integral part of our lives. These jobs have such titles as customer service representative, reservation agent, ticket and gate agent, account representative or executive representative, telemarketing representative, technical support representative, and eligibility and claims specialist. They are in industries as disparate as manufacturing, insurance, banking, travel, and retail. Many handle more than 100 customers per day. They must be conversant with a variety of databases that collect and store the information required to perform the job.[25]

Ellen's job is considered one of the best call-center jobs. It pays more than other centers because it is in the airline industry, which is highly unionized. The vast majority of call-center workers are in jobs that pay less than $8.50 an hour.[26] Ellen's job is also a step up from workers who have to call out to people to try to sell them a product. Here, the customer comes to you. But all these jobs are high-pressure and stressful. Workers are forced to balance service to the customer with employer pressure to meet a sales quota in an atmosphere of constant surveillance.

CHILD-CARE WORKER

Sharon Bright helps educate children at a day-care center for underprivileged children. During the summer months, when the children are not in school, she works from 12:00 P.M. to 7:00 P.M. and during the school year from 3:00 P.M., the time the center opens, until closing time at 7:00 P.M. There are only four day-care workers for fifty children. Sharon evaluates each child's reading and math levels and works with them to improve their skills. She supervises arts and crafts, sports, and games, and takes the children on field trips to museums.

"Many of the children use degrading language with each other. I try to improve their self-esteem and work to improve the respect they have for each other. It's a real challenge. A lot of kids just don't like themselves," she says. In many cases, Sharon acts like a surrogate parent. She is there when they need to talk, when they need a hug, when someone hurts their feelings. During the summer, she also helps prepare lunch and dinner for the children. Many times these are the only meals the children will have that day. She tries to ensure a balanced diet, but it is difficult because money is short and she must rely on donated food. "It takes a long time to prepare food for fifty children," she says. "It is not like cooking at home."

Because the pay is low—Sharon makes $7.50 an hour—turnover is high. "But you have to build trust to be effective," Sharon says. "When you work with the same students every day, you understand them, their habits, and what they need. The day-care worker informs the parent about the child's developmental milestones, whether they see any problems, and whether there are emotional issues that need to be addressed. If there is a constant turnover of workers, it is hard to know a child's history.

"When you work with children there are no breaks," she says. "It is nonstop. It is not like working in an office where you can leave for thirty minutes and clear your head." Sharon is lucky if she gets a five-minute break. She can't leave the children alone, and there is no one to replace her.

The job requires a lot of patience. "You have to be willing to do whatever it takes to answer any questions the children ask. You have to like children and be active with them. It is not a sit-down job. A day-care worker must be able to relate to the children: the things going on in their neighborhoods, the music, the slang, their interests. You don't have to like what the children like, but you have to know about it and be able to screen what is inappropriate."

. . .

Educating and caring for young children pays low wages. Of the over three million child-care workers, including family child-care providers, more than 80 percent earn less than $8.50 an hour. One-third of the workers earn less than $5.75 an hour.[27] The 1.2 million teacher's assistants do no better. And these occupations are expected to grow in the next ten years by over 400,000.[28] This workforce—98 percent of whom are female—has a higher concentration of jobs that are paid below the official poverty line than almost any other occupation in the United States.[29] These jobs are clearly important and the workers skilled and educated; indeed these workers are better educated than the general population.[30] Almost a third of the child-care workers and teacher's aides have a college or advanced degree, and 44 percent have some college. But because of the low pay, there is a 30–40 percent average annual turnover rate in the industry that hurts the quality of care provided to our children.[31]

JANITOR

Flor Segunda, the Newark janitor, cleans the sixth-floor law offices of a suburban New Jersey commercial office building. She has cleaned the same offices for eight years. Her shift begins at 6:00 P.M. When she first arrives at work, she goes downstairs to the office, punches her time card, signs in, and gets her keys for the twenty offices she cleans. She then goes to the sixth floor, gathers her two carts—one for recyclables and the other for trash—and begins pulling garbage from each office. Once the carts are filled, she takes them to a large barrel on her floor, which she first cleans of yesterday's spilled drinks and old food. She then lines it with a plastic bag before dumping her cart of trash into the barrel. When the carts have magazines, binders, or boxes full of paper, they can weigh as much as thirty pounds. She has strained her back several times lifting them.

She gets done with the trash at about 8:00 P.M. She then begins cleaning the individual offices on her floor. She dusts the desks, tables, chairs, bookcases and any artwork in each office. She washes the lawyers' coffee cups. "People are pretty messy," she says. "Some offices have papers, clothing and shoes all around the office. I know that certain lawyers want me to straighten it up. They leave a note thanking me. The advantage I have being there a long time is that I know what the tenants like, whether to leave things alone or clean up. The lawyers leave purses, wallets, laptop computers in their offices because they know me. We have confidence in each other," she says.

After she finishes in the individual offices, she puts on gloves and cleans the glass on the doors, the marble tables, the kitchenette and the watercooler with ammonia. The ammonia is very toxic. She once got it in her eyes while cleaning a window above the door.

At 9:50 P.M., she turns off all the lights and goes downstairs. She then punches her time card and rushes to catch the bus to go home. In order to catch the 10:00 P.M. bus, she has to leave a few minutes early. She constantly struggles with her supervisor to let her have those couple of minutes. If she doesn't catch the 10:00

P.M. bus, she must stand alone at night and wait the twenty minutes for the next bus. "I'm scared," she says.

·   ·   ·

In the growing business services sector, there are over two million janitorial jobs. Some are porters who work at lobby desks during the day, but most are like Flor, who clean offices in the evening. Three hundred thousand janitorial jobs are expected to be added in the next ten years.[32] Two-thirds of the janitors earn less than $8.50 an hour. And 22 percent, or one out of five janitors, earns less than $5.75.[33] Twenty hours per week is the maximum number of hours most janitors can obtain. Even at $8.50 an hour, a janitor working twenty hours earns less than $9,000 a year. Most janitors have second jobs because they cannot afford to live on the income from their night janitorial job. Because of the low pay and difficult night hours, there is a high turnover rate. Unlike Flor, who has worked in the same building for eight years and has established ongoing relationships with the tenants in the building, most workers leave within a year. Of the thirty-four workers in Flor's building, only seven have been there more than one year and only two people have been there more than five.

POULTRY-PROCESSING WORKER

The noise is deafening. The floors are slippery with chicken grease. The smell of chicken blood fills the air. Workers standing in pools of water, hang, slice, split, pull, and cut chickens at breakneck speeds of ninety-one birds per minute. Standing close together in their hair nets, gloves, coats and boots, they wield knives in temperatures ranging from freezing to 120 degrees. The plant runs twenty-four hours a day, working three continuous shifts. Workers are on the line six days a week, sometimes seven. These are the jobs that put chicken on our tables.

Bob Butler, the Albertville, Alabama, poultry processor, has seen almost all the jobs in his plant. "The toughest and most dangerous job," he says, "is live hanging." The workers grab live chickens with their hands. While the chickens peck, scratch, claw, and defecate on them, the worker shackles the chicken by the legs. Feathers fly and the birds screech. The stench from the birds never leaves one's nostrils. Grabbing and shackling the chickens must be done at breathtaking speeds—one bird every two seconds.

Once the chickens are hung, a machine cuts their throats. But if the machine doesn't do it properly, a worker cuts the chicken's throat with a knife, sending chicken blood everywhere. The chickens then go through scalding water that removes their feathers. The next machines sever their heads and feet.

The hot chickens then fall onto a transfer table where four workers, two on either side of the table, rehang the chicken by grabbing their legs and flipping them onto shackles. The small work space and 100-degree temperatures create a "nasty smell," Bob says. "The closest I can come is when an animal is killed on the side of the road and has been lying there for several days. It is worse than that."

Once the chickens are rehung, they continue on a conveyor belt where workers open the chicken with their thumbs and yank and twist out their guts with their hands. During this process, the workers must make sure the chicken's gall bag doesn't break. Otherwise the chicken will be ruined. The trimmer, who sits next to the U.S. Department of Agriculture inspector, checks the chickens for any bad areas and either cuts them off or takes the chickens off the line. A machine then cuts the heart and livers, but the workers determine whether they are edible. A worker then pulls out the gizzards with his hands while another worker ensures that the gizzards are clean and free of intestines and lungs. A trimmer then cuts off the neck bone.

After the evisceration line, the chickens are chilled for ten to fifteen minutes and dropped once again onto a table. The chiller hangers then grab the freezing chickens with their hands and flip them onto shackles. Next, workers in thirty to forty degree temperatures, standing elbow-to-elbow in water, slice the chicken into parts. It is so noisy from the machines that workers must wear earplugs to prevent hearing loss.

Twelve workers standing on a catwalk then grab the chicken breasts, thighs, drums, and wings and put them into a bag. They must pack seventy-five breasts a minute. Workers' hands swell from the constant grabbing motion, and tendonitis is common.

After the chicken is packed, a worker weighs it and sends it to a shaker table that vibrates the meat to settle it before the box is closed. A worker then tapes the boxes and sends them down a belt where a worker stacks thirty to forty boxes on a pallet, six to eight feet high. A shipping worker wraps the pallet with plastic and loads it on a truck or drives it to the freezer for storage. To avoid frostbite in the freezer, he wears a face mask and protective clothing.

·   ·   ·

There are more than 200,000 poultry processing jobs in the United States. Because of strong consumer demand for chicken, it is one of the fastest-growing segments of the meat industry. Over the last ten years, the dollar value of poultry production has more than doubled from nearly six billion to twelve billion dollars.[34] Poultry production employs more workers than any other segment of the meat industry, growing from 19,000 workers in 1947 to today's 200,000 workers.[35] Although an essential job, poultry processing workers suffer poor wages (75 percent earn less than $8.50 an hour), minimal benefits, and harrowing working conditions.[36] Their counterparts in the meat and fish industries face the same harsh conditions.

HOME HEALTH-CARE AIDE

The phone call came in. Joann Morris's coordinator had a new client for her, a fifty-one-year old woman with multiple sclerosis. Her name was Millie. She was incontinent and couldn't walk. Because her tremors were so forceful and continuous, she could rarely control her hands or arms, and her speech was slurred. That was six years ago.

Joann is a home health-care aide. In addition to the training required to be state certified, she takes continuing in-service programs to maintain her certification. In a home-based setting, Joann provides personal and physical care for the elderly, disabled, patients with serious health problems, or those recovering from surgery.

Joann has been with the home health-care agency for ten years. Her first patient was a woman with arthritis, diabetes, and cataracts. She was homebound and incapacitated. Her second client had a type of arthritis that caused her to bend over so far her hands almost touched the floor. Her third client had Parkinson's disease. She also cared for two homebound AIDS patients when a fellow aide was ill.

When Joann arrives at Millie's apartment at 8:30 A.M., she first sits and talks with her, washes her hands, and changes Millie's adult brief diaper. Joann then gives Millie a bed bath; a regular bath would be too dangerous. She gets the materials ready: a basin, water, soap, two washcloths, and towels. If Millie can do her own genitals, she encourages her to do it. "It gives her a feeling of being in charge of her own body and a sense of independence," Joann says. Millie's skin is very tender, so she has to be careful. After the bath, Joann applies powder or lotion.

After dressing Millie, she prepares breakfast and gives Millie her daily medications. Afterward, Joann moves her to a wheelchair with a mechanical lift. "It is good for her circulation and well-being for her to get up," Joann comments. "Bed-bound patients easily get bedsores. If untreated, they get deeper and deeper and can ultimately cause death."

She is very careful when she moves her. She rolls Millie on her side, straightens the lift pad, takes the S hook and connects it to the pad and makes sure it is locked in place, and then pumps the lift and guides her head and pushes the lift over the wheelchair and guides her down. She continually observes Millie to make sure she isn't dizzy or afraid. "One misstep could be a disaster," she says.

When Millie is in her wheelchair, Joann serves her lunch, a meal that she herself rarely has time to have. She helps with Millie's bills and letters and then changes the bed linens that get soaked with urine when Millie leaks through her diaper at night. She turns the mattress once a week and airs it out with a little Pine-Sol. Millie likes the smell. "Every patient is different in what they like," she says. "I try to buy colorful sheets instead of drab hospital colors. I try to make her life as bright and cheerful as I can."

She then sweeps, mops and dusts the apartment and does Millie's laundry. If there is a doctor's appointment, Joann takes her. If Millie wants to nap, she uses the lift to get her back in bed. While she is asleep, Joann prepares her dinner, confers with the nurse about Millie's prescriptions, readies her nightly medications, and tidies up the kitchen and refrigerator.

Once Millie gets up, she changes her adult diaper briefs and prepares her for dinner. Most of the time, Millie likes to eat in private. "Her shaking embarrasses her," so Joann leaves the room. Sometimes she needs to talk. She needs a shoulder. It is really hard for her. After dinner, Joann kisses her on the forehead. She tells her God bless and have a good evening, and then she leaves to go home at 5:00 P.M. After she leaves she usually shops for Millie's groceries, clothes, and other household needs for the next day.

·   ·   ·

Home health-care aides and nursing aides provide for the well-being of our elderly and disabled in individual homes and nursing home settings. Yet two-thirds of the home health aides and nursing aides are paid less than $8.50 an hour.[37] Home health-care work is often part-time, which exacerbates the already low wages. These poor wages result in turnover rates of 40–60 percent. And in nursing homes, the inadequate staffing on top of these meager wages produces turnover rates of 70–100 percent. With constant turnover, experienced aides bear a greater patient load, which produces an even greater burnout rate. This vicious cycle is found throughout the nursing home and home health-care industries.

Home health-care and nursing aide jobs are two of the fastest-growing occupations in the health-care sector, a sector that accounts for half of the fastest-growing occupations in the U.S. economy. One out of five jobs created in the nonfarm economy since January 1988 has been in health services.[38] As patients shifted from hospitals to less expensive alternatives such as nursing homes and home settings, there was an explosion of home health-care and nursing aide jobs. The number of home health aide workers, now over 600,000, is expected to increase by 300,000 in the next decade. During that same period, the field of nursing aides, orderlies, and attendants, now at approximately 1.3 million, is also expected to add another 300,000 jobs.[39]

GUEST ROOM ATTENDANT

Sylvia Mendez is a hotel guest room attendant. She makes sure that the beds we sleep in, the toilets we use, and the showers where we wash on a business trip or family vacation are clean. Sylvia works the day shift from 8:00 A.M. to 4:00 P.M. After arriving at the hotel, she gets her cart. She fills the cart with linens, towels, cleanser, furniture polish, soaps, and magazines for the sixteen rooms she cleans. Full, the cart weighs over two hundred pounds, making it difficult to push. Once it is loaded, she pushes it out into the hallway and goes to her first room. When she enters the room, she always leaves the cart across the open door for safety. Guest room attendants have been accosted while cleaning the rooms.

Sylvia first strips the linens from the bed and picks up the towels from the bathroom floor. "They make a real mess," she says. "There is trash all over the room. People leave beer bottles on the tables, and towels and papers all over the floor. They think if they pay for it they can just leave everything. They don't care. But it's impossible to finish sixteen rooms when they are really nasty."

After she picks up the trash, towels, and linens, she makes the bed. The sheets must be wrinkle-free. The blankets and the bedspread follow. Once a month, she must turn over the mattress. She then dusts the furniture in the room. She takes a rag with Windex or water, depending on whether it is glass or wood, and cleans the tabletops, chairs, dressers, side tables, and paintings in the room. She vacuums the carpet. She then organizes the magazines and the menus and places them on top of the table next to the telephone. She makes sure everything is dusted and cleaned and put properly in its place.

She then cleans the bathroom. "People leave greasy stuff all over the bathtub," she says. "There is urine on the toilet and the floor." She mops the floor and then scrubs the toilet on her hands and knees. She then scours the shower doors, the countertops, the sink, and the bathroom mirror with a cloth. She replaces old soaps, shower caps, and shampoos. To finish all sixteen rooms, many days she takes no breaks or lunch.

·   ·   ·

The more than 400,000 hotels and motels in the United States provide rooms to millions of business and family travelers every day.[40] Guest room rentals account for three-fifths of the $50 billion in total hotel and motel receipts. The guest room attendant's job is essential to ensuring that these rooms are properly cleaned and maintained for hotel and motel guests. Yet more than 80 percent of the one million guest room attendants, like Sylvia, get paid less than $8.50 an hour. Over 350,000 workers get paid less than $5.75 an hour.[41] And many of these workers work irregular and part-time schedules. For nonsupervisory workers in the hotel industry, the average workweek is 30.4 hours, four hours less than the private industry average.[42] At $8.50 an hour, this amounts to less than $14,000 a year. In slow periods, employers cut hours without notice, reducing these workers' already meager wages.

PHARMACY TECHNICAL ASSISTANT

Judy Smithfield works in a superstore as a pharmacy technical assistant, a "pharmacy tech." Her 12:00–9:00 P.M. shift begins with a call from a nurse in a doctor's office dictating a prescription over the phone or a customer at the counter giving her a prescription. Once she has the information, she gives it to the pharmacist to process in the computer. Then it is Judy's responsibility to check that information and get the proper medication from the shelf. She counts the pills that are prescribed, puts them into the bottle, affixes the proper label to the medication, gives the filled prescription to the pharmacist for her review, and puts it in the proper bin for the customer to pick up.

Once the customer arrives, Judy must ensure that she has the right prescription and that the proper forms are filled out. She must ask the customer whether they understand the prescription, whether they want counseling or have any further questions. Their response must be put in writing.

Three times a week, Judy receives the drug orders that are delivered to the store. "They must be put in the place designated so there is no confusion in filling prescriptions," Judy emphasizes. "It is essential." The pharmacist must sign for controlled substances, but Judy fills these prescriptions.

It can get very busy at the pharmacy counter, especially during flu season. If someone has to wait twenty minutes for a prescription that they just brought in, they get angry. "They say, 'All you have to do is put pills in a bottle. What takes so long?' They don't understand that we must follow procedures to ensure accuracy," Judy says. When people get impatient and angry, Judy has learned to apologize a lot. But sometimes that doesn't work. "Sometimes they get real upset," she says.

There are two pharmacy techs and three pharmacists on Judy's shift that fill over 400 prescriptions per day. If the pharmacy gets behind in the prescriptions, Judy stays late, sometimes until midnight. Many times she works six days a week because they don't have enough help. Her feet and back ache from standing all day.

· · ·

Judy is part of the large retail sector. More than 21 million Americans, one out of every six workers, currently holds a retail job.[43] From 1979 to 1995, the number of jobs in retail grew 39 percent, resulting in almost six million new employees.[44] And another 2.3 million are expected to be added in the next five years.[45] Retail workers serve customers at drugstores, department stores, rental counters, and grocery stores. They are salespersons, cashiers, stock clerks, counter and rental clerks, and pharmacy assistants. Many perform some of the same functions as Judy, waiting on customers, stocking products, and answering customer questions. Her pay, like the rest of the retail industry, is low. Three-fourths of the retail jobs pay less than $8.50 an hour.[46] Compounding the low pay is the frequency of part-time schedules. Thirty-eight percent of retail employees work part-time.[47] As a result, nearly two-thirds of the non-managerial workers earn less than $12,500 per year.[48]

RECEPTIONIST

Nancy Holland's day begins at 8:30 A.M. when she picks up and distributes faxes and the more than thirty Audix messages that have come in after hours to the receptionist desk. She then opens the switchboard to receive incoming calls. During the day, there is an average of 600 to 700 phone calls. "I try to be as helpful as possible to them and talk very slowly and make sure I am directing them to someone who can assist them so they won't have to call back," she says.

While Nancy is receiving calls, she opens the president's mail, sends it to his office, and receives, sends, and distributes faxes. She handles the general mail of the organization and marks it for distribution. She files, processes letters, works on the computer, and assists shipping when they need help in mail-outs. She stuffs envelopes, manages the chronological files for the president's secretary, and fills in when secretaries are on medical or personal leave.

And every day she receives visitors to the organization. "When someone comes in, I put my best foot forward to be pleasant and helpful. It is important to their overall view of the organization. I am a part of making people who come to our organization feel good about the people they are going to see and potentially that will help better our business.

"The toughest part of my job," says Nancy, "is being tied to a desk all day. I can't get off the desk unless I have someone to relieve me. It is very restrictive. There are people coming in all the time, so it has to be covered continuously."

• • •

Nancy's job is one of the many jobs that support business operations. Her job is crucial to how outsiders view the company. In many instances, if someone has a good impression it is greatly determined by how Nancy performs her job, whether she is polite and friendly, whether she knows who has the information being requested by a caller or visitor, and whether she assists these people in a professional manner. Her job also facilitates internal operations by circulating information, performing clerical functions, and supporting other departments within the organization. Yet, a majority of the 1.5 million receptionists earn less than $8.50 an hour. The number of jobs in this field is expected to increase by over 400,000 in the next five years.[49]

• • •

These low-wage jobs are the backbone of the new economy. Yet, just as Americans misunderstand and undervalue these low-wage jobs, they misconceive who works in these jobs. Their misconceptions help them dismiss the problems faced by these workers. It is important, therefore, to understand who these workers really are and who must reap the consequences of jobs that provide so few rewards.

CHAPTER 4

The Demography of a Caste

Who are America's low-wage workers? Many presume they are teenagers, illegal immigrants, or high school dropouts. These images perform a useful psychological function by allowing us to dismiss this phenomenon as one of societal outliers. Yet contrary to these stereotypes, America's low-wage workers are mostly white, female, high school educated, and with family responsibilities.

THE BASICS

Teenagers comprise only 7 percent of the low-wage workforce. Indeed, it is adults, a majority of whom have families, who labor in these jobs.[1] And it is young adult non–college graduates who saw the most dramatic erosion of their wages over the last thirty years, with males earning 25 percent and women 13 percent less than their 1973 equivalents.[2]

Nearly two-thirds of the low-wage workforce is white.[3] Yet, blacks and Latinos are overrepresented in this group relative to their participation in the overall workforce.[4] In fact, the proportion of minority workers in 2001 earning a low wage is substantial: 31.2 percent of blacks and 40.4 percent of Latinos in contrast to 20 percent of white workers.[5]

Women make up 60 percent of the lower-paying workforce, even after a slight decline over the past two decades.[6] Almost 30 percent of the female workforce is low-wage, in contrast to less than 20 percent of the male workforce. Of these women, three-fourths are white. Yet the proportion of minority women is significantly higher than white women: 35.8 percent and 46.6 percent of black and Latino women in contrast to 26.2 percent of white women.[7]

This is not to downplay the number of men involved. In fact, men have increased their share of low-wage work over the past twenty years, reaching close to one-fifth of male workers.[8] While they comprise 52 percent of the workforce, they still make up only 40 percent of the low-wage workforce. The statistical story for white men is similar. While white men have increased their share of the low-wage workforce over the past 20 years, they still hold fewer low-wage jobs proportionately than women and minorities.[9] Women of color are four times more likely to hold a low-wage job than white men. White women are three times as likely as men to hold a low-wage job. And men of color are one and a half times as likely as white men to do so.[10]

When it comes to education, it is not surprising that the low-wage workforce has less formal education than workers in more highly paid occupations.[11] But contrary to the common belief that most low-wage workers lack a high school education, 40 percent have a high school diploma, 38 percent have at least some postsecondary education, and 5 percent have a college degree.[12]

The low-wage labor force overall is better educated today than it was a generation ago. This mirrors the increase in education in the general labor force. The proportion of all workers with at least a college degree, for example, increased from 19 percent to 31 percent between 1979 and 2001. At the same time, the proportion of those without a high school degree fell from one in five to one in ten.[13]

BEYOND THE BASICS—A STEEP HIERARCHY

It is no accident that women and minorities command a disproportionate share of low-paying jobs. Discrimination in the U.S. workplace has historically played a role in excluding them from higher-paying positions.[14] While women and minorities made significant advances in the past generation with the creation of equal pay and equal opportunity legislation in the sixties and seventies, discrimination persists.[15] With the same education, income continues to be lower for nonwhites and women.[16]

Even within the low-wage sector, historically disadvantaged groups occupy the lowest rungs of the system. White males earn more than white females, and white females earn more than both black and Latino males and females with the same skills and jobs.[17] And employers link race and gender with job suitability that locks in this stratification in the low-wage workforce.[18]

So what is the situation for women workers today? Certainly, things have improved. The disparity between men's and women's wages dropped by 15 percent during the past thirty years.[19] Yet women still have lower incomes and are more likely to work in low-wage jobs than men with similar qualifications.[20] Nearly 60 percent of full-time female employees are paid less than $25,000 a year, and nearly 70 percent of the full-time female labor force is in low-paying occupational categories.[21] While women had some success moving to traditionally male jobs in white collar and service occupations, they met with little such success in blue collar jobs including higher paying precision, production, and craft occupations.[22]

Even within the low-wage sector, women are still concentrated in a number of low-status, low-paying jobs that are generally typecast as "female" jobs.[23] Women, for example, make up close to 70 percent of the low-wage salesclerks and service workers.[24] And native-born minority and immigrant women continue to disproportionately hold jobs in private households that are more likely to pay and provide the fewest benefits.[25] This occupational segregation hurts women.[26]

Female-dominated occupations pay less in spite of the fact that female-dominated occupations have more workers with college coursework. Women low-wage workers in general have higher levels of education than their male counterparts.[27] Childcare workers, who are almost all female, make less than animal trainers, who are largely male.[28] And these jobs provide less training and fewer advancement opportunities than male-dominated occupations.[29] Women, in fact, represent 76 percent of the workers in jobs with the fewest advancement opportunities and only 5 percent of those in jobs with the most.[30] It is not surprising that women are less likely to move out of low-earning jobs than men.[31]

And low-wage occupations that employ mostly women have more part-time hours and temporary work than other jobs. Women comprise over 70 percent of the regular part-time workforce that constitute one-fifth of the overall workforce.[32] Beyond regular part-time work, women make up 60 percent of the three million temporary-help industry jobs, including agency temps, direct-hire temps, on-call workers, and day laborers, a majority of which are low-wage.[33]

Women with children face added barriers to getting better jobs. Today, 65 percent of married women with children under the age of six and 75 percent of women with school-age children (ages six to seventeen) work outside the home, triple and double the number, respectively, since 1960.[34] Since 1979, the number of hours worked by couples with children increased by 600 hours, reflecting the overall increase in hours worked by women outside the home.[35]

Despite the dramatic increase in the number of working mothers, the structure of America's workplaces and the family-support systems in place since the fifties have barely changed. Heidi Hartmann and Vicky Lovell with the Institute for Women's Policy Research (a leading research group on women's labor market issues) describe this stagnancy as "imposing an enormous disadvantage on women who wish to combine their labor market and caregiving work."[36] This is in sharp contrast to Western Europe, where family policies such as family leave,

child care, government-supported preschools, and increased
workplace flexibility were introduced to accommodate the in-
flux of working mothers to the workforce.

American workers get less government support for child care
than any other country in the industrialized world, making
child-care costs relative to women's earnings higher in the
United States.[37] Until passage of the Family and Medical Leave
Act in 1993, the United States had no national maternity leave
policy. Even now, it is tied with Switzerland in offering the
shortest period of leave among the thirty democratic, industrialized nations comprising the Organization for Economic Cooperation and Development. It is one of the only OECD countries
that does not offer some amount of pay during that period.[38]

The American workplace is still organized around what
American University law professor Joan Williams calls the
"ideal worker." This is someone who can work forty hours a
week, all year, with required overtime, and take little or no time
off for childbearing or child rearing. Women who are still primarily responsible for caregiving and men who have child-care
responsibilities cannot live up to this ideal.[39] Instead of changing working conditions to adjust to the new reality, the U.S.
workplace treats mothers like men without child-care responsibilities.[40]

But without family-supportive policies and a restructured
workplace, women, who continue to bear the primary responsibility for childcare and elder care and are more likely to be cus-
todial single parents, are forced to reduce their work hours, take
breaks from employment or avoid jobs that are likely to require
work schedules that would clash with their family responsibili-

ties.[41] High-paying jobs in the manufacturing sector, for example, provide few opportunities for part-time or flexible schedules. In fact, many require overtime that essentially excludes most working mothers.[42]

Instead, three-quarters of working-class women must take traditional female jobs that offer more flexible schedules.[43] Yet in doing so they sacrifice pay and benefits and must work more nonstandard hours. One-half of young mothers with less education work evenings or night shifts or on weekends. In a cruel irony, this makes it more difficult to care for their children.[44]

The limited choices mothers face results in what Columbia professor Jane Waldfogel aptly labels the "family gap."[45] While young women without children earn 90 percent of men's wages, mothers earn only 60 percent.[46] The United States has the largest "family gap" among industrialized countries.[47]

Despite these barriers to working mothers, little attention has been focused on the need for change. The long-held assumption that men are the principal breadwinners of families and that spouses are merely providing "pin money" and are somehow less reliant on their wages and benefits still curbs the urgency for reform.[48] This assumption, however, is inconsistent with the facts. Women's incomes are essential to the well-being of low-income families. Women in many married couples are the sole support of the family. In 1993, one out of every five married couples was supported solely by the wife's income, an increase of 14 percent from 1980.[49] Among married couples, women contribute on average one-third of the family income.[50] And women are the sole earners in nearly two-thirds of families maintained by a single person.[51]

Minorities face other obstacles to better-paying jobs. While lower levels of formal education among African Americans and Latinos hamper their prospects, discrimination still plays a large role.[52] Nonwhites with comparable levels of education earn less and are less likely to be working than whites.[53] Within occupational groups, race plays a role in determining job levels and thus factors such as pay, benefits, and the degree of autonomy on the job.[54]

And minorities hold a disproportionate share of the low-wage temporary-help industry jobs with black workers twice as likely to hold these jobs as whites. More than 20 percent of the agency temp workers are black, yet they represent only 12 percent of standard full-time workers and Latinos are twice as likely to be on-call workers than whites.[55]

Hiring discrimination continues to plague inner-city African-American males. Many employers prefer whites, black women, and Latino immigrants to black males.[56] This discrimination excludes them from the "better" jobs frequently found in manufacturing and from suburban jobs where employers serve predominately white clientele.[57] But according to Harry J. Holzer, Georgetown professor of public policy and a leading expert on minority labor market issues, "not all types of employers discriminate equally." [58] Small establishments, a large proportion of the American workplaces, are some of the worse offenders.[59]

Yet it is immigrants who generally work in the lowest rungs of the low-wage workforce. Amendments to the immigration laws in 1965 began a new wave of immigration to the United States, principally from Latin America, the West Indies, and Asia.[60] Between 1970 and 1996, the number of foreign-born increased by fifteen million, rising from 4.8 percent to 9.3 percent of the U.S. population.[61] By the mid-eighties, 600,000 new immigrants were coming into this country each year.[62] And today, one out of every five children in the United States lives in an immigrant family.

This increase in the immigrant population had a significant effect on the workforce. Between 1996 and 1999 alone, the number of foreign-born workers employed in the labor force increased 17 percent from 13.4 million to more than 15.7 million.[63] Three-quarters of these immigrants live in six states: California, New York, Texas, Florida, New Jersey, and Illinois.[64] In California, over 30 percent of the working-age population is foreign-born.[65] And these figures do not include the eight to nine million undocumented workers that the 2000 census suggests are currently in the United States.[66]

These new immigrants work in a wide array of jobs, but they are more likely than natives to work in the harshest jobs in the low-wage workforce. Forty-three percent of foreign-born workers were employed in low-wage jobs in 1997. The economic gap between today's immigrants and native-born workers is three times larger than it was during the last major wave of immigration at the turn of the century.[67] Male immigrants today typically earn only 77 percent of what natives earn, with Mexican-born men earning less than half.[68]

Immigrants are more likely than natives to be food-preparation workers, sewing machine operators, parking lot attendants, housekeepers, waiters, private-household cleaners, food processing workers, agricultural workers, elevator operators and janitors, operators, fabricators, and laborers.[69] Almost half of all housekeepers are immigrants.[70] In states where there are large immigrant populations, such as California and New York, three out of four textile workers are immigrants.[71] These occupations have the greatest number of jobs that pay below $8.50 per hour. Few of their employers provide health insurance, pension plans, sick leave or family leave, and these jobs have the least advancement possibilities. One in three Latinos, for example, are not insured through their employers.

Immigrants are funneled into some of the most hazardous and unhealthy jobs, such as roofing, trench digging, and carrying heavy materials. Latino immigrants, for example, die from workplace injuries at a 20 percent higher rate than either blacks or whites.[72] And the lack of training and instruction in their native language on safety and health in these hazardous workplaces aggravates this situation.[73]

Certainly, English-language proficiency and educational barriers play a part in limiting immigrant job options, especially for a notable proportion of Latino immigrants. Only half the Mexican immigrants have attended secondary school, and only one-third have graduated.[74] This minimal education prevents many immigrant workers from gaining certain higher-paying positions. And the lack of English proficiency disqualifies them from jobs that require reading or communication skills.[75]

But there is a more pernicious reason why immigrants face the most abysmal conditions—their vulnerability. Immigrants are less likely to know their rights, and undocumented workers fear deportation if they complain about workforce abuse. Some employers, in fact, illegally recruit undocumented workers.[76] As University of Missouri sociologist William Heffernan, who studies the meat processing industry, notes, "This has been around for a long time in the meat processing industry. Employers can take advantage of these people because they can threaten to send them back." [77]

This same exploitive strategy occurs in other industries. A 1998 Department of Labor study determined that two-thirds of Los Angeles and three-quarters of New York garment factories that employ a large proportion of immigrants violated wage laws. [78] Many undocumented workers were working forty-eight hours and making $180 per week. These conditions have been largely ignored, leaving immigrants in the worst and most abusive jobs.

·   ·   ·

Workers with less education find it difficult to find quality jobs in the United States. Yet, in spite of an increase in white males into the lower end of the labor market, there still exists a caste-like system with women, minorities, and immigrants at the bottom of this labor force. They face this situation with little ability to provide for their families and with little hope of movement in a society that practically worships the concept of social mobility. Who does this hurt? Certainly the workers. But there are other consequences to these workers' children, our society, and to all of us standing by.

CHAPTER 5

How Low-Wage Jobs Damage Us All

Why should we care that over thirty million Americans and their families face these conditions? We should care because it is morally repugnant. In a nation as rich as ours, where CEOs make four hundred times the average rank-and-file worker, leaving workers without the basic protections of life should be unthinkable. While one can argue that certain individuals should receive larger rewards than others for their contributions to society, it is quite another story to leave those who have worked hard without even the minimal necessities.

Allowing these conditions to continue challenges our notions of basic equity and fairness as these workers play by the rules and get so little in return. It erodes our most cherished values of personal responsibility, hard work, and perseverance. It sends the message that work does not pay. It may be that so little has been done to rectify this problem because of who these workers are. Yet if America does nothing to address these conditions, it locks this hierarchy in place and threatens to make it not an aberration of American society, but a norm of the American economy.

But it is not on these grounds alone that we should care. There are costs to these workers' families and to society as a whole. Leaving a large group of workers out of society's rewards impairs the functioning of America's democracy and communities and destroys the kind of nation we want to become. Our country is growing more fractured, with an increased social distrust and a lack of confidence in government and in each other. Letting these conditions fester damages our nation's economy and aggravates society's social ills. Ultimately, allowing these conditions to persist undermines the country's moral foundations and in the process diminishes us all.

THE COST TO CHILDREN— A FATE, NOT A FUTURE

Low-wage jobs are hard on children. They are the unseen victims of these low-wage jobs.

Unlike the elderly, whose poverty rate has halved since 1970, childrens' poverty rates are higher today than they were three decades ago.[1] Nearly 17 percent of children in the United States live in poverty—more than thirteen million children.[2] These poverty figures exceed those in most other advanced countries, ranging from 1.5 to four times higher than in Canada and Western Europe.[3]

Looking only at the number of children "officially" in poverty, however, underestimates the extent of the problem.

Family income for children in the bottom one-third of families is 16 percent lower than a quarter of a century ago.[4] And millions of children suffer similar deprivations, even though their parents' incomes put them slightly above the "official" poverty rate.

Children of low-wage workers start off at such a deficit that it calls into question our belief in "equal opportunity." And the stakes are higher today. Workers who have not completed high school or have a postsecondary education suffer greater economic penalties than they did in the past.

Conservatives have historically focused on "equal opportunity" as an essential core American value rather than "equality of outcome." But that focus fails to grasp that the meager outcomes for the thirty million low-wage workers diminishes the equality of opportunity available to their children. "The pay of America's lowest lifetime earners has become so remote from the pay of the median earner as to make them a class apart, with radically diminished possibilities next to those in the mainstream," Columbia University economist Edmund Phelps explains. "The gulf in pay, by sapping their initiative and hindering their access to middle-class institutions' casts a pall over poor communities and leaves a legacy of disadvantage for the next generation."[5]

As conservative University of Chicago economist James Heckman so aptly notes, "Never has the accident of birth mattered more. If I am born to educated, supportive parents, my chances of doing well are totally different than if I were born to a single parent or abusive parents. I am a University of Chicago libertarian but this is a case of market failure. Children don't get to 'buy' their parents and so there has to be some kind of intervention to make up for these environmental differences." [6]

The impact of inadequate income on a child's health, education, emotional and behavioral development, and occupational attainment can no longer be questioned. Parental income is the single most important factor in accounting for differences in the socioeconomic attainment of children. [7] Low income alone is strongly correlated with a low level of preschool ability, which subsequently leads to lower test scores, grade failure, school disengagement, higher dropout rates, and less successful adult careers. [8] And lower-income children are at a higher risk of mental health problems, depression, low self-confidence, peer conflict, and conduct disorders than children from parents with higher incomes. [9] This has been recently corroborated by a study at the Joint Center for Poverty Research at Northwestern University. [10]

All of this is common sense. Without adequate resources, parents are forced to live in poorer neighborhoods with higher crime rates and social problems. [11] Flor Segunda's and Linda Stevens's children face these conditions daily. Each day Linda's daughter must steer clear of the gangs hanging out on the corner. They also move more frequently, which hurts their children's education. [12] "It is hard on my oldest son, who is in grammar school," Flor says. "Each time we move, it takes time for Jose to adjust. He has to make new friends. It hurts him in school."

The working poor have the least access to high-quality early-childhood services. [13] Without subsidies, these parents are forced to piece together child care with relatives, friends, neighbors, or low-cost family day-care centers. [14] And subsidies from the government are difficult to obtain. Estimates are that only 12 percent of the almost fifteen million children eligible for child-care subsidies actually received them in 1999.[15] As *New York Times* reporter Sara Rimer notes, "Low-income working families are in many ways the forgotten class in the national debate over child care. They make too little to afford the choices of professional women, whether to use a nanny or an au pair, to work part-time or full-time. Many make too much to qualify for government programs. Others make little enough to qualify, but are low on long waiting lists while priority is given to women leaving the welfare rolls for jobs." [16]

Children need a stimulating environment for normal brain development, and without that stimulation, children's psychological and neurological development can be irreversibly impaired.[17] Studies show that children in low-quality child care behave more aggressively, react poorly to stress, and have delayed cognitive and language development.[18] They are more likely to drop out of school, repeat grades, need special education and become delinquent.[19] Many low-income parents have no choice but to place their children in substandard arrangements.[20]

Without adequate child care and family resources, poorer children start public school less prepared. Low-income parents have trouble affording books and computers.[21] Their children must depend on the schools to catch them up and provide the necessary educational tools. Yet, many schools in poor neighborhoods lack the resources to offset these differences in school preparation.[22]

More money is spent to educate more affluent children.[23] Although researchers differ over the degree that money matters in educational outcomes, most agree that it does have an impact.[24] They all agree, moreover, that certain parental resources help children succeed in school: the ability to identify and choose good schools and school districts, the ability to live in a good neighborhood, the ability to provide formal and informal educational resources at home, and a high degree of parental education—resources that many children of low-wage workers lack.[25]

To further compound their difficulties, children of lower-wage workers are less healthy than those of higher-paid workers.[26] They are exposed to more environmental risk factors: lead paint, rundown housing, crime, pollution, and family stress. They are less likely to be covered by health insurance than children from more affluent parents.[27] Some children qualify for government programs such as CHIP or Medicaid. Yet ignorance of eligibility for these programs (many believe one must be on welfare to qualify) and bureaucratic hurdles, including lengthy and complicated application forms, prevented more than half of parents from enrolling their children in 1998–1999.[28]

A child's health improves with health insurance coverage.[29] Uninsured children have a higher rate of acute and infectious diseases and have a higher number of hospitalization stays.[30] They are six times more likely to go without needed care, five times more likely to use a hospital emergency room as a regular source of care, and four times more likely to have necessary care delayed.[31] Being sick makes it difficult for any child to have consistent school attendance and good school performance. For children of low-wage workers, however, it adds yet another barrier for these children to overcome.

Children of low-wage workers get less parental time and supervision than children of parents in higher-wage jobs. Their parent's jobs provide fewer vacation days and holidays, less family leave and sick leave, and many of their parents must work two jobs or overtime hours.[32] The lack of time off and job flexibility deprives these workers' children of parental care when they are sick, have a problem at school, have an emergency, or just need the day-to-day attention that all children require.[33] The lack of adult care and supervision has a lasting effect. These children are less likely to finish school and are more likely to be delinquent.[34]

If children of lower-income workers succeed in high school, in spite of these many obstacles, they are still half as likely to attend college as students comparably qualified from the top income group.[35] The gap between college-entry rates for low-income families and high-income families is as wide as it was three decades ago.[36] High school students from low-income families who had high scores on standardized tests were less likely to attend college than all students from the top income group.[37] Yet even when children attend the same schools, the disparity persists.[38]

The economic importance of postsecondary education has risen dramatically in the last two decades. In 1980, the average twenty-five- to thirty-four-year-old male college graduate earned 19 percent more than the average high school graduate of the same age.[39] Twenty years later, the difference had nearly tripled.[40] And for women today, the differential is even higher, reaching 60 percent.

Most students have responded by staying in school longer. But this response is directly correlated with family income. From early 1980 to the mid-nineties, the number of high school seniors from the top quarter of income earners who went to a four-year college increased by over 10 percent. In fact, the large increase in college enrollment in the past twenty years was among children in the top 60 percent of income.[41] By contrast, college enrollment in poorer homes showed no change.[42]

The future trend for lower-wage children is not promising.[43] Aid programs for the poor have fallen off. Most programs do not give enough to get a student from a low-income family through a two-year community college without a struggle.[44] A report by the Advisory Committee on Student Financial Assistance found:

> The opportunity to pursue a bachelor's degree is all but ruled out for increasing numbers of low-income students by record levels of unmet need. . . . Over the past three decades there has been a shift in policy priorities away from access at all levels that has caused a steep rise in the unmet needs of low-income students. As a result, the cost of higher education has risen steadily as a percentage of family income *only* for low-income families, while middle income affordability and merit have begun to displace access as the focus of policy makers at the federal, state and institutional level.[45]

The decision to leave these children without help also has social costs. We all pay for the impact of these conditions on the workers' children. Schools pay when they must invest added resources to offset the lack of readiness. Our economy suffers when these children grow up to be less educated and productive adults. Taxpayers pay for all the problems in the form of higher expenditures for schools, social services, medical care expenses, and criminal prevention.[46] But ultimately society pays with more crime, less social cohesion, and decreased participation in our communities.[47]

COSTS TO OUR DEMOCRACY

Lower-wage Americans today are the least likely to participate in the democratic process.[48] In the last forty years, the proportion of Americans who vote in elections has dropped by more than 10 percent, placing it close to the bottom among democratic countries.[49] The low voter turnout, however, is not random among economic groups. Voting has fallen most sharply among those with lower incomes.

Corporations and individuals with money can make political contributions that influence government decisions. As mass communication and marketing have become preeminent in elections, money to pay for television and marketing has become increasingly more important, skewing even further the influence of those with money. That influence is reflected in legislation and government regulation that favors corporate interests and wealthy individuals who can contribute lavishly. Those without resources have little to offer that can compete.[50]

"People in Washington, they're trying to make decisions and they're making top dollars and here we are trying to get by and they want to give us minimum wage," Cynthia Porter explains. "They just don't get it. Why vote?" Under the best of circumstances, the enormous demands on low-wage workers make it difficult for them to participate fully in the democratic process. But the lack of rewards from the system alienates them from the process and produces a cynicism about participating.

What does this portend for the future of our democracy? What happens when a large group of citizens withdraws from the democratic process? Our democracy is premised on a reasonable degree of equality amongst its citizens. This equality brings a commonality of focus, values, and participation. As class distinctions become more pronounced and certain groups withdraw from the process, American democracy as we know it will disappear.

COSTS TO FAMILIES

This country extols the institution of marriage and the primacy of family values. Yet, the economic hardship and financial instability many low-wage workers' families face puts added strains on their domestic life. Increased domestic violence is one result. Higher divorce rates and lower marriage rates are another. Intact families living in poverty dissolve at double the rate of families above the poverty level.[51] When the wages of white men in the bottom two-thirds of the labor market stagnated or fell between 1973 and the mid-nineties, their marriage rates declined. By 1996, there were dramatic differences in the marriage rate between this group and the top one-third of wage earners.[52] Conversely, with better economic prospects, marriage rates increase and domestic violence rates decrease.[53]

The same positive correlation between better jobs and marriage rates was found to be true in the African-American community. Harvard sociologist William Julius Wilson determined that the decline in black men's labor market prospects was a key to the disintegration of the black family. Beginning in 1970, as the number of marriageable men and those with steady jobs fell in low-income communities, women in these communities became less likely to marry.[54]

The lack of positive job prospects for both men and women without a college education also leads to a greater number of teen pregnancies.[55] Experts suggest that less educated women faced with few reliable providers as spouses and few prospects of their own do not postpone having children.[56] In fact, they believe they have relatively little to lose by having a first birth in their teens or early twenties. The incentives for postponing parenthood are only substantial for young women when they really believe that they have a strong prospect for making it into the middle class.[57] Having intact families is especially important to children, as children in single parent households suffer the highest poverty rates.[58]

COSTS TO OUR COMMUNITIES

Low-wage jobs hurt America's communities by reducing the taxes for local schools and other public services. Examining the impact of a living-wage ordinance in Santa Rosa, California, a recent study by Sonoma State University sociologist Peter Phillips found that increasing the wages of low-earning workers would in fact produce substantial new spending in the Santa Rosa local economy that would benefit local businesses.[59] Likewise, increasing the wages of low earners would infuse needed money into low-income neighborhoods.[60]

With a decrease in economic opportunities for workers, America's communities also face increases in alcoholism, drug addiction, and crime.[61] Policing, peer effects, neighborhood conditions, and the severity of penalties certainly influence the propensity for individuals to commit crimes. Yet better employment prospects also play a part and, like sanctions, affect the incentive to commit crimes.[62] In the eighties and nineties, for example, depressed labor markets for less educated men contributed to a rise in their criminal activity. Likewise, crime rates decreased in the late nineties as unemployment in the low-wage sector fell and wages increased in a full-employment economy.[63] As Harvard economist Richard Freeman notes, reducing youth crime rates would be made easier "by enhancing the rewards for legitimate work." [64]

Taxpayers also pay for the increased costs of crime and other social ills in the form of a costly criminal justice system. A staggering number of American men are involved in crime compared to other industrialized countries. Roughly 3 percent of the male workforce is incarcerated and about 9 percent is under supervision of the criminal justice system. By the mid-nineties, one man was incarcerated for every fifty men in the workforce.[65]

Mass incarceration is an expensive way to control crime. Taxpayers pay $20,000 a year to house and feed every new inmate, about as much per year as sending someone to a good university. Seventy-four billion dollars is spent on the criminal justice system.[66] In 1995, California alone budgeted more for prisons than for higher education.[67] The cost of inadequate jobs is a growing prison and jail population and a costly criminal justice system. Ensuring that Americans have good jobs is one part of a larger strategy for reducing crime and limiting the costly strategy of mass incarceration.

COSTS TO OUR ECONOMY

Improving productivity is essential to our economic growth. This becomes even more imperative as the size of our workforce declines over the next twenty years. As Harvard economist David Ellwood points out, "In the last twenty years, our prime labor force—people between twenty-five and fifty-four—grew by 20 million, 16 million of them native born. In the next twenty years, the growth of that labor force will be zero." [68]

Increasing productivity requires that employers make investments in workers in the form of training and technology. These are investments that most low-wage employers fail to make. To the contrary, the conditions in these jobs inhibit rather than enhance job performance. As the Work and Family Institute noted in its *1997 National Study of the Changing Workforce,* "When workers feel burned-out by their jobs, when they have insufficient time and energy for themselves and their families, when work puts them in a bad mood—these feelings spill back into the workplace, limiting job performance." [69]

With so few rewards, there is little incentive for lower-wage workers to remain on these jobs. These high turnover rates drain productivity. [70] When a company continually needs to replace employees, costs are increased and sales are lost because new workers need to be hired and trained. [71] The high number of absences due to worker accidents and illnesses that result from these jobs diminish output further. These demanding jobs and un-supportive workplaces also reduce the productivity of future workers.

These low-paying jobs reduce economic growth by reducing the consumption of goods. More than two-thirds of American gross domestic product is based on personal consumption and 85 percent of that consumption is in consumable goods and services.[72] The failure of these jobs to provide adequate wages constricts the purchasing power of these workers and, in turn, decreases the gross domestic product.

In spite of the disadvantages to our economy, many businesses continue to use this low-wage, high-turnover strategy. The conventional thinking has held that low-wage workers are plentiful in supply, interchangeable, and easily replaced.[73] But this strategy overlooks the demographic changes that will occur in the next twenty years that will significantly reduce the supply of labor. In a tight labor market, these low-road policies are more difficult to employ.

Whether or not an individual company can succeed, however, is not really the point. Individual companies have gained competitive advantages by polluting streams or hiring child labor. But many have worked over the years to condemn and make such practices illegal. Laws have attempted to prevent companies from benefiting from these actions. The same should be true here. While an individual business may benefit from these low-road policies, it is not in the interest of our overall economy or society.

Continuing these vast inequalities and low-road policies,

more-over, undermines the very rationale for our economic system. One of the leading experts on U.S. income distribution, MIT economist Frank Levy explains, "Our markets are justified not only on the basis that they enhance individual freedom, but that the economic growth they create helps everyone."[74] The free market today fails that test for more than thirty million Americans.

COSTS TO CONSUMERS

Employers defend the practice of keeping labor costs down in these low-wage jobs as a means of keeping down costs to consumers. No doubt, Americans have gotten more inexpensive services and goods as a result. Yet as a nation do we really want to enrich ourselves by exploiting other workers? Beyond the moral question, there are trade-offs to Americans consumers. We learned that when airlines auctioned off airport security to the lowest bidder—creating some of the lowest-wage, poorly benefited jobs in America—American lives were risked. After September 11 there was a move to improve airport security by improving the wages, working conditions, and training for the women and men who staff these jobs.

This is a lesson that can be applied more broadly. There are millions of low-wage jobs in the United States, which may not suggest the urgency of airline safety, but do supply some of our most essential needs. The same lesson applies. The level of wages and benefits that these workers receive and the working conditions in which these workers operate directly affects the quality of the services they provide. This is basic common sense.

As Princeton economist Alan Krueger succinctly puts it, "Economic logic says you usually get what you pay for." [75]

A variety of studies establish the inextricable link between the wages, benefits, and conditions of a job and the quality of the service provided.[76] A study of pre–9/11 airport security directed by Michael Reich of the University of California at Berkeley examined the impact of a quality standards program at the San Francisco International Airport. The San Francisco program, begun in April 2000, established compensation, hiring, and training guidelines. Starting pay rose from $5.25 to $10 an hour plus health benefits, or $11.25 an hour without benefits. The average wage in the industry was $6.00 an hour. Not surprisingly, turnover decreased from 110 percent to 25 percent. Employers reported that absenteeism and grievances fell as morale, skills, and performance improved.[77]

Other studies that focus on the nursing home, home healthcare, and child-care industries show similar results.[78] In each of these industries, poor wages, insufficient benefits, and poor conditions create large turnover. Effective care for the elderly, the disabled, or a child requires consistent interaction with the same provider of care who is knowledgeable about the adult or child. Yet annual turnover rates for nursing assistants—who supply nearly 90 percent of the care in most nursing homes—can be as high as 100 percent. The inability to earn a sufficient income to support their families (nursing home aides make, on average, $7.93 per hour with few benefits) makes these workers leave their jobs.[79]

In a report to the Maryland General Assembly, which examined the quality of Maryland's nursing homes, the authors cited nursing home staffing, pay, and training as the key ingredients in improving the care in the state's nursing homes.[80] The Health Facilities Association of Maryland, an industry trade association that represents 154 nursing homes, concurred in this assessment of how to improve care: "Stabilizing the workforce of direct caregivers is one of the most important things that can be done."[81] The findings are consistent with studies of nursing homes throughout the United States.[82] To improve nursing home quality, the treatment of workers must improve.

A study of home health-care workers found the same connection between improvements for workers and improvement in the quality of service.[83] When home health-care workers were provided with better wages and benefits, there was a dramatic reduction in the job turnover rate, which is the key indicator of quality service.[84] The Cooperative Home Care Associates, a worker-owned home health-care agency in New York employing over 450 workers, pays 20 percent more than the area average of $7.65 an hour. They provide health benefits and compensation for aides' travel time to their clients. In contrast to the industry norm of seventy-five hours, CHCA provides four weeks of training. They also try to provide full-time work and career advancement opportunities. The result has been a job turnover rate of less than 20 percent in an industry where turnover reaches 60 percent.[85]

"If we want 'quality care' to mean truly competent, individualized, and compassionate care," Rosalie Kane, a University of Minnesota professor and a prominent authority on long-term care, notes, "we must find a way to provide 'quality jobs' as well. If we allow current circumstances to prevail, if we permit the majority of caregivers to remain poorly paid, unappreciated, and poorly supported, we will also have made our choice about what we can expect for those in need of care."[86] The same linkage is seen in other industries. Artie Nathan, vice president of human resources at the Mirage hotels, credits the low turnover in his casino hotels, 70 percent in an industry that can run as high as 300 percent turnover, to the better wages and training they provide the workers.[87]

Inadequate rewards and harsh working conditions also contribute to low worker morale, worker anger, and disaffection. As Donna Klein, vice president of workforce effectiveness at Marriott International notes, "The ironic thing is that the quality of our product and the delivery of service are driven by employee mood."[88] It is pretty basic. The delivery of quality service in a job is related to how a worker is treated in that job.

COSTS TO OUR NATION'S HEALTH

The association between income and health is long-standing. The poor have worse health than the near poor, the near poor fare worse than the lower middle class, the lower middle class fare worse than the middle class, and the middle class fare worse than the upper class.[89] The lowest economic groups have a higher incidence of cancer, heart disease, diabetes, asthma, and respiratory disease and have a greater likelihood of death from illness or injury than other groups.[90] This is consistent with the increased risk for hypertension, cardiovascular disease, and mental illness from work environments that offer little autonomy or control and are concentrated in low-wage occupations.[91]

New, striking research postulates that the more unequal a society, the more unhealthy is not only the poorer group but the general populace.[92] The entire society suffers. The size of the gap in income and assets between the top and bottom of a society can itself be an important determinant of the health of all members of a society. Once nations achieve a minimum threshold of income, economic inequality is strongly related to the population's mortality and life-expectancy rates.[93] The United States, the world's wealthiest nation, performs poorly on major health indicators, ranking close to the bottom among wealthy countries in average life expectancy.[94]

Harvard public health professors Ichiro Kawachi and Bruce Kennedy hypothesize that the connection between economic inequality and a society's poorer health and higher mortality rates stems from economic inequality's effects on a society's decreased social cohesion and the erosion of its social capital. This lack of social capital includes the decrease in interpersonal trust between citizens, norms of reciprocity, and the vibrancy of civic associations.[95] Diminished social cohesion leads to under-investment in public education and other forms of social spending. University of Sussex professor Richard Wilkinson finds that economic inequality produces poorer health outcomes because "more unequal societies are marked by higher levels of violence, lower levels of trust, more hostility and less involvement in community life."[96] What is clear from this recent research is that the conditions of low-wage workers in America may contribute not only to their poor health, but also to the poor health of our society as a whole.

·   ·   ·

If these workers become the invisible "other" that we ignore, it is a tragedy not only for the workers and their families, but those standing by unwilling to act. It changes us as we sit by, accommodating this inhumanity. We become numb to those around us as we distance ourselves from the connection that binds us to other human beings. We close off the caring and compassionate parts of ourselves. It is our loss.

If we want a society in which our citizens participate, one that is supportive of families, one with healthy and productive people, one with safe and thriving communities, and one in which every individual can reach his or her fullest potential, we must act to change these low-wage conditions, which our society has helped to create. Yet as we look to make improvements, we must not allow common myths to blur our vision and prevent us from seeing clearly.

CHAPTER 6

An Apology for Indifference

Myths can supply simple answers to complex problems. They can also be used in a more pernicious way to undermine our determination to act and avoid the truth. Four myths have dominated the debate over low-wage work. The first is that low-wage jobs are merely a short-lived step on a ladder to a better job. The second is that improving skills is the primary solution to the problems of low-wage work. The third is that because our companies compete in the global market, we are unable to act domestically to improve the lives of these workers. And the fourth is that volunteerism is a substitute for social policy. These myths blind us to other forces that underlie many of the problems of lower-wage work and function less as explanations than as excuses not to act.

THE MOBILITY MYTH

One reason why many people are not more sympathetic to the plight of low-wage workers is the belief that enduring the harshness of these jobs is temporary, that mobility will take care of the problem. These workers will either move up to a better position in their current jobs or move on to better jobs. The Horatio Alger myth is a centerpiece of American culture. If someone fails to rise, it must be his or her own fault. It must be a product of lack of will or diligence, just as success is the result of individual hard work and perseverance.

But this belief belies the reality. Mobility will not bring significant advancement to most low-wage workers. At a time of rising income inequality, mobility is declining or, at best, staying the same. Boston College economist Peter Gottschalk examined mobility between 1974 and 1991 and found that of those workers in the lowest 20 percent of income earners in 1974, almost 70 percent were in the same group the next year and fully 91 percent were in the bottom 40 percent.[2] A similar study conducted by Gottschalk and University of Michigan professor Sheldon Danziger found that even after twenty-five years, close to 50 percent of those in the bottom 20 percent of income had not moved beyond that income group. Of those who had moved, half had only moved to the next highest wage group, still below the median wage.[3]

Low-wage jobs, historically, have had few career ladders. Today they offer even fewer.[4] In many industries as diverse as insurance, retail trade, restaurants, information technology, financial services, airlines, and health care, there is a segmentation of the labor force between those who serve the lower- and higher-income markets.[5] The result of that segmentation is a stratification of service jobs associated with each submarket and fewer job ladders for lower-wage workers to move into higher-paying jobs.[6] At the same time, small wage increases coupled with job instability provide few opportunities for low-wage workers to improve their current jobs.[7] It is no wonder that it is harder today for young workers to move into the middle class.[8]

In fact, contrary to the American assumption that the United States has greater mobility than other industrialized countries, an OECD study found that the United States economy had less mobility for low-earners than France, Italy, or the United Kingdom.[9] Even compared to countries with more centralized wage-setting institutions like Germany, Denmark, Finland, and Sweden, the United States still had less mobility for low-earners.[10]

It is true that a small number of workers move on to better positions, generally outside the low-wage sectors.[11] These better-paying jobs, however, are mostly in manufacturing, a sector with a declining job base. Still others use these jobs as a means to finance their college tuition. But for the vast majority of workers, their situation is permanent.[12] Mobility is blocked, not because these workers lack motivation or diligence, but because there are few paths to better jobs.

SKILLS WILL SOLVE THE PROBLEM

How do we solve the problems facing low-wage workers in this country? "Reskilling" is a nearly universal response. In this economy, the argument goes, workers cannot make a livable income because they lack the requisite skills needed for the new technological jobs. The changing skill requirements of the economy have created a "skills mismatch."[13] It is the uncon-

tested "truth" of our day. Former Secretary of Labor Robert
Reich reflected this widespread belief early in the Clinton administration.

> Like comparable periods before, our current era of rapid
> economic change opens new opportunities. Every Ameri-
> can can develop the skills to make it in the new economy.
> . . . The payoff to skills is surging. Technological evolution
> is spawning a profusion of good new jobs. Integrated, ex-
> panding global markets create many more opportunities
> than they close off. And the skills needed for many of these
> high-skill, high-wage jobs can be learned. . . . [14]

This belief translates into a bipartisan cry for better education
of future workers and reskilling those already in the workplace
for our economy's "high-tech," "high skill" jobs.

The "skills mismatch" theory is a significant overstatement
of the demand for high-skilled workers. Skill requirements are
growing at only a modest rate and are expected to continue to do
so in the future.[15] In 1996, 53.5 million workers—40 percent of
the total workforce—worked in jobs requiring only short-term
on-the-job training.[16] The overwhelming majority of occupations require only a high school education or less. Occupations
generally requiring postsecondary training accounted for only
3 out of 10 workers employed in 1996.[17]

Certain high-tech jobs, especially in the manufacturing sector, go unfilled because employees lack the requisite technical
skills. The number of those jobs, however, is quite small when
compared to the lower-wage service sector and the manufactur-

ing jobs for which improved "skills" may have little impact in overall working conditions. And providing training for high-tech jobs does not create jobs requiring those skills.[18]

This new economy has, ironically, increased the share of lower-wage employment, not lowered it. While there has been an increase in managerial and professional jobs, there is also more demand for lower-wage jobs today than two decades ago. From 1965 to 1998, the two lowest-paying sectors, retail and service, increased their share of employment from 30 percent to 48 percent of all production and nonsupervisory employment.[19] The middle-paying sectors of our economy have lost shares. In 1963, 37 percent of all production and nonsupervisory workers were employed in the three middle-paying sectors of the economy. During the same time, the bottom three sectors employed 35 percent of the workforce. By 1998, however, the share of the three middle-paying sectors of the economy had dropped to only 16 percent of the workforce, while the bottom three sectors rose to 63 percent of the workforce.[20]

And lower-wage service jobs are expected to have the largest growth. Put another way, in the next ten years, half of all new jobs will require only short- or moderate-term on-the-job training. This includes: nearly one and a half million new jobs in the food preparation and food service occupations; one million in retail sales and cashier occupations; another million in health-care support occupations; and nearly one million in cleaning and maintenance occupations.

So why has the skills solution gained such preeminence? Talk of our "new economy," even in the wake of the bursting dot-com bubble, creates the impression that high-tech jobs are the largest occupational group. The media and experts focus on the new computer-based jobs. It is not news to speak about jobs that have been in the labor market for a long time, such as nurse's aides, child-care workers, hotel workers, and janitors. Confusion between the percentage of job growth of some new jobs and the actual number of jobs in these occupations adds to the belief that high-tech jobs have taken over our economy.

The number of computer software engineers and computer-support specialists will double between 2000 and 2010 while cashiers will increase their share of employment only 14 percent.[21] But new positions in these computer-service occupations generate large growth rates because they are relatively new fields with smaller numbers of employees. By 2010, there will be less than 1.8 million of these software engineers and computer-support specialists, while there will be nearly 3.8 million cashiers.[22] Low-wage job growth will dwarf these high-tech jobs.

The low end of the job market will account for more than 30 percent of the American workforce.[23] Employers will hire nearly twice as many food-service workers as software engineers, hire as many cashiers as they do computer-support specialists, and hire more than twice the number of customer-service representatives as they do computer-systems analysts.[24] The jobs that have substantial contact with people and are less immediately affected by technological change will have substantial job growth.[25]

The labeling of these jobs and the workers in these jobs as *low-skilled* has given further credence to the skills solution.

Skills have been defined in terms of educational level or technical expertise, generally related to the ability to use computers. But this notion overlooks the types of skills possessed by child-care workers, nursing home workers, or hotel workers—skills of patience, caring, conscientiousness, and communication.

If our concept of skills is redefined to include activities such as the attention to detail that a maid must have in order to clean a hotel room properly, the psychological and emotional support that a nursing home worker or home health-care worker gives to our parents, the educational and social enrichment that a child-care worker or educational assistant provides our children, the knowledge and courtesy that a call-center worker gives us when we order products or ask questions regarding our accounts, and the conscientiousness and dedication of a security guard ensuring our protection in our workplace, then the contributions of these workers can be fully valued.

On a more fundamental level, the skills solution has gained such widespread support because it provides an easy answer to a much more complex set of questions. According to the reskilling thesis, the problem is the fault of the workers themselves. Individuals need to improve themselves through skills development. It asks little of employers, politicians, or our society. Employers escape scrutiny about why these jobs are so poorly rewarded. Politicians avoid dealing with the more politically thorny issue of how these employers share their profits with their employers, and it gives them cover for lowering government supports or not having to create any new ones in the future.[26] Once workers are educated or reskilled, the argument goes, they will be able to fend for themselves.[27] And we as a society are freed from having to look at the ground rules that make it so difficult for these workers to succeed.

This is not to downplay the importance of education reform and workplace training. Having a more educated populace in our dynamic global economy is obviously important. It makes our nation more productive and competitive. And for lower-wage workers and their children, it is essential to ensure an equal opportunity for them to compete. Workers with more education generally hold higher-paying jobs than those with less.[28] Even for many jobs that require only a high school education, one or more cognitive or social tasks such as reading, writing, and dealing with customers or computers are needed.[29] Today, some students, especially black and Latino males, are hampered in their job prospects because they lack these skills.[30]

Similarly, workers must be given opportunities to continue the learning process once they have entered the workforce. Today, however, the probability that workers receive workplace education is directly proportional to their wage and education levels. This leaves lower-wage workers the least likely to receive any employer-sponsored training.[31] Without workplace education, these workers lack the means to improve skills in their present jobs and to gain new education that would increase their chances of moving into higher-paying jobs.[32] This must be changed.

Certainly, raising skills will lead some workers to higher wages. But this reskilling approach will do little to improve the lives of most workers in these low-wage jobs, jobs that will continue to grow as a proportion of our economy. What these workers need is to be adequately rewarded for the skills they already possess.

GLOBALIZATION MAKES US DO IT

Global trade with both industrial and industrializing nations has had a profound impact on our economy and on American workers. Most dramatic has been the increase in trade with less-developed countries, rising from less than one-seventh (14 percent) of all U.S. trade in 1970 to almost triple that amount today.[33] During this same period, the growth of average wages in the U.S. slowed, and the wage levels of workers with less than a college education fell.[34] While economists and policy makers disagree as to the extent of globalization's impact on this decrease, most all agree it played some role.[35] Increased trade with less developed countries eliminated jobs in the manufacturing industries where the products compete globally, such as textiles, shoes, data input, cars, and steel.[36] Three million manufacturing jobs were lost between 1979 and 1999.[37]

Globalization's impact on the manufacturing sector also has an indirect effect on the service sector. The combination of the depressed wages in the manufacturing sector, more competition for service jobs from displaced manufacturing workers, and new job entrants who are unable to find manufacturing jobs, puts downward pressures on wages and benefits for jobs in the service sector.[38]

As profound as the impact of global trade has been on our economy, it does not, as some argue, preclude low-wage employers and our society from improving the wages and working conditions for lower-wage workers.[39] Only a small portion of low-wage jobs are actually in industries that compete globally.[40] While globalization has had a large impact on the manufacturing sector, these manufacturing jobs account for only a minority of today and tomorrow's lower-wage workers.[41]

This is not to say that no service jobs compete globally. Transportable skills such as data input and information technologies have been filled abroad. There are call-center workers in English-speaking countries answering our questions and taking catalog orders. Just across the border, 45,000 Mexicans work in data-processing and other service jobs. One can also imagine lower-wage food-processing jobs being shipped overseas or across the border.

But most lower-wage jobs are and will continue to be in the non-tradable service and retail sectors.[43] Checking out groceries, waiting on tables, servicing office equipment, protecting airline passengers, caring for children, tending the sick, and cleaning up for the rest of us must take place in a specific location where the child, patient, or customer is present. These jobs cannot be shipped overseas. While the poor wages of workers in China or Bangladesh depress the general world wage structure and have an indirect effect on U.S. workers, workers from less-developed countries are not in direct competition with nursing home, child-care, security, or hotel workers.

In spite of this reality, employers and politicians use globalization as an excuse for doing little or nothing for lower-wage workers. Many employers use the threat of global competition to justify decreasing their employees' wages and benefits and cutting jobs. This includes employers who, in fact, are not competing globally. They scare their workers into accepting less.

Workers, continually bombarded with the globalization message, believe they are powerless to act, regardless of whether their job is in a non-tradable sector. If they push for higher wages, they fear they will lose their jobs. But if they do nothing, their wages continue to stagnate. Political conservatives invoke globalization as a reason for reducing social spending.[44] They argue that any employer obligations will make U.S. companies uncompetitive in world markets.[45]

This globalization rhetoric also deflects our attention from the political and business choices that account for the plight of these workers, choices that have little to do with the global marketplace. It makes it appear that external forces beyond our control cause the problems of lower-wage workers. Nothing is further from the truth. Other industrialized countries competing in the same global markets as the United States have made political and business choices to ensure that all workers can rely on a safety net. As a result, workers in similar jobs in other industrialized countries have fared far better than American workers.[46] Low-income Americans have living standards that are 13 percent below that of low-income Germans, 17 percent below low-income Belgians, and 24 percent below the average income of the bottom 20 percent of Swedes. This is despite the fact that the median American enjoys a standard of living far above the median German, Belgian, or Swede.[47]

As a group of prominent economists from the Brookings Institution and the Progressive Policy Institute note, "The bottom line is that while trade may amplify the total losses and gains, societies still face the fundamental decision of whether or not to grant the social protection: if it makes sense to offer the protection in a closed economy, it will also make sense in an open economy."[48]

This is not to take lightly the injustices of unrestrained trade. As a nation, we must determine under what circumstances trade should continue. Will it benefit only business and the wealthy, or will it also benefit working Americans? What are the rules in which world trade should take place? As the International Labour Organization Director-General Juan Somavia argued before the World Trade Organization in Seattle: "I don't believe you can shut off globalization. It is a reality. But there are ways to make it much better for people than it is now."[49]

Today's unrestrained global trade must be addressed, yet globalization should not be used as an excuse for failing to rectify the problems of lower-wage workers.[50] If we refuse, it will not be because of outside forces. In the words of long-time-MIT, now-Princeton economist Paul Krugman, "We cannot evade responsibility for our actions by claiming that global markets made us do it."[51]

VOLUNTEERISM AS SOCIAL POLICY

With the advent of the George W. Bush administration, a new myth in old clothing has arisen—faith-based voluntary solutions. It is the belief that volunteerism, particularly through faith-based organizations rather than social policy, is the answer to these problems.[52] The United States has a long and well-recognized history of volunteerism, and it will always have an important place in our society. Voluntary organizations provide many essential services and resources to people in need, many of whom are in dire circumstances. But volunteerism cannot be a substitute for social policy.

It is commendable that overburdened food banks and homeless shelters try to provide food to the hungry and a place to stay to families who have nowhere to sleep. If jobs paid a living wage, however, these families would have a greatly reduced need to use these services. If working Americans and their children had access to health insurance coverage, there would be less need for free clinics. If low-wage parents had the resources to provide quality child care and after-school care and jobs that provided the needed flexibility to properly supervise their children, less teen delinquency and school dropouts would result. If jobs provided adequate rewards, there would be less hopelessness that drives many to drugs and alcohol.

This is not to say that there are not individuals who make poor choices or those who cannot take care of themselves for reasons beyond their control. This is not a call to eliminate individual responsibility or volunteer organizations. But if working Americans had the resources and time to properly care for themselves and their children, many of the problems charities deal with today would be less severe.

Focusing on the effects of the problem rather than the problem itself once again deflects attention from the societal structures we have chosen. It serves as a way of deflecting attention from the failure of our society to provide good jobs and a basic safety net to all Americans. In so doing, it shifts responsibility from the private and public sectors to the individual to find a way to cope with the social ills caused by these deprivations.

But when millions of Americans cannot properly feed, clothe, shelter, and provide their children with the basic amenities of a healthy childhood, it is not merely the problem of the individual. When more than forty million Americans lack health insurance, it is not just an individual problem. At a time of historically low unemployment, the demand for charitable services increased dramatically—not decreased. The U.S. Conference of Mayors found that emergency food assistance alone grew 18 percent between 1998 and 2000, fueled by working people.[53] This is not a situation in which a few people cannot take care of their basic necessities. It is a problem with the system.

Volunteerism as a policy is flawed for another important reason. Americans who work hard should not have to rely on handouts for their basic necessities. They should not have to rely on the goodwill of individuals and organizations to make up for the deficits of their jobs. By forcing people to rely on voluntary organizations, their plight is continually uncertain. The voluntary sector is small in comparison to the need, and many are set up to provide emergency assistance, not ongoing services.[54] But more importantly, if work does not provide the means to care for oneself and one's family, hard workers are put in the unseemly and degrading position of having to beg for help from a homeless shelter, the Salvation Army, or a food bank.

Volunteerism is also bad social policy. Failing to address the problems that cause many of these social issues is costly to our society. It is more difficult to solve the problems that result from inadequate income, lack of parental time to supervise one's children, poor-quality child care, and lack of health insurance than to deal with the deficits of low-wage jobs. Dealing with drug abuse is more difficult and intractable than dealing with improving lower-wage childrens' access to quality child care. Failing to address the issues up front, society pays the larger costs in increased crime, drug addiction, and poorly performing children.[55] This is not to say that these problems will vanish if we ensure that working families have the basics to thrive. But attacking the structural deficits underlying many of these problems would be far more productive than merely trying to deal with the fallout.

. . .

We must move beyond these myths. These workers face a world in which they have little power to change their conditions. Their inability to improve their conditions is a result of our creation, not natural law. It is this world that we need to enter.

CHAPTER 7

A Question of Power

It started when the company told the workers that it was eliminating their two fifteen-minute paid breaks. A half hour of pay is a major wage cut for workers making only $8.20 an hour. In a poultry processing plant, where workers are constantly cutting, pulling, slicing, and hanging chickens at breakneck speeds, arm to arm in deafening noise, a break is a necessary reprieve.

Things had been building up to this point. The company had threatened to take their paid breaks away the year before and only relented when workers threatened a strike and called a union. But there were other problems at the plant. After repeated complaints, workers still weren't allowed to leave the line to go to the bathroom. One of the oldest male workers had messed in his pants and "it went all the way into my boots. The most humiliating part was going home to my wife and her friend who happened to be visiting."

There were only five commodes for more than 600 men. It got so bad that fights broke out in the bathroom. When workers complained about the problem at a meeting, the company responded, "I'm sorry we can't provide nice plush marble bathrooms for you."

Workers were also getting hurt. The most prevalent problem was carpal tunnel syndrome, a painful debilitating condition that makes it nearly impossible to use one's hands. When workers asked to slow the lines, they were told that if they didn't like it they could leave.

"They are also mean to the people," one worker said. "This boy, his aunt died on a Wednesday but he didn't find out till Thursday. They were burying her on Friday. So he asked the supervisor if he could be off to attend the funeral. The supervisor said, 'Hell no, you ought to have told us yesterday if you wanted the day off.' "

Employing 1,200 workers, the poultry processing plant is the largest employer in a town of 23,000 people. More than 80 percent of the workers are Latino, most of whom are Guatemalan and had come to this formerly all-white town in the hills of Georgia specifically to work at the plant. Few if any other job opportunities are available to them in the town, where Confederate-flag decals are still prominently displayed on pickup trucks. There was a Klan march two years ago.

But when the company announced that they were eliminating the paid breaks, the workers balked. They were determined to walk out, and a local Spanish-language newspaper reported the news. The union that the workers had called the year before when the company initially threatened to eliminate their paid breaks came to their aid, but armed with warnings.

They would face huge obstacles, said the union. The company

would use all of its multimillion-dollar resources to stop the workers from organizing. The company would hire a law firm. It would probably threaten to bring in the INS. The workers would get little support from the townspeople, while the top officials in town would be aligned with the company.

Despite these warnings, the workers wanted to proceed. But nothing could have prepared them for what happened once they filed a petition for an election to have the union represent them. The company hired a law firm known for its hardball tactics, the police were called out, and police cruisers were stationed inside the gates of the plant. Some of the plainclothesmen were dressed in suits, while others wore long coats and cowboy hats. To many of the Latino workers, they looked like the INS. The workers were so frightened that 300 people didn't show up for work.

The company began checking workers' identification at the entry gate and only the maintenance men—who were primarily white—were exempted. The company began filming workers who were taking handbills from other workers. And then they fired one of the leading activists in the organizing effort.

Workers were required to attend weekly company meetings, one for the Latino workers and one for the white workers. The company told the white workers that the union would take away their health insurance and they told the Latinos that the INS would check everyone's papers. Both groups were told that the union was just after their money. The company said, "These people are down here now, but you will never see them after this. We are the ones that look after you."

Videos of violent strikes were shown at the weekly meetings, though the company didn't mention that those strikes involved an entirely different union. The videos showed a woman getting hit with a bullet, cars shot at, and concrete blocks being thrown through windows. The company enlarged the picture of the injured woman and hung it in the plant.

The company told the workers they would never negotiate with the union. As one worker said, "I thought the company would close the plant. I was frightened. I have someplace to go, but most people don't. I've stuck my neck out to get the union. I am nervous if the union doesn't get in I will be fired."

At the same time, the company began to allow workers to do the things they had prohibited before the petition was filed. They allowed workers to leave the line to go to the bathroom. To increase the number of men's commodes, a women's bathroom was changed into a men's bathroom. They made efforts to accommodate particular workers. For the first time, a union supporter, who had a limp and a bad back, could park in a handicapped parking space.

As the election date neared, supervisors handed out "Union-No" T-shirts. Workers were told that if they didn't wear the T-shirt, they would not be a part of the company. The day before the election, supervisors bought lunch for a group of workers who had recently come from remote areas of Guatemala and spoke a dialect that limited their ability to talk to other workers. They wrote *no* on the workers' hands. The union lost the election.

Charges were filed protesting the company's actions, but any resolution will take months or even years. Even if they are successful, the most that will probably happen is another election. Despite a few cosmetic changes, conditions remain the same.

. . .

These poultry processing workers, like most low-wage workers throughout the United States, have little power to create better working conditions. As opposed to workers in many professions, they have no ability to limit the flow of workers into their market by restricting entry and reducing competition. And without union representation or resources, most low-wage workers have no ability to spell out their employers' obligations in a contract or to influence government policy on their behalf.

Instead, low-wage workers are in the most open markets in the United States with the least power to control employment conditions. As a result, during one of the longest periods of prosperity in this country, they reaped few real benefits. Between 1973 and 1993, the real income of the lowest 20 percent of workers fell as much as 11.7 percent.[1] It was only at the end of the nineties, during one of the tightest labor markets in recent history, that these workers finally saw wage increases. And low-wage men still did not see their real inflation-adjusted incomes reach their 1979 levels. As a final insult, these workers were the first to lose their jobs and suffer reductions in hours due to the 2000 economic downturn.

Too many economists, policy makers, and politicians would assert that the plight of these workers is merely the work of an efficient market, a matter of supply and demand. It is one of the great illusions of markets, however, that they appear to work without human agency. This illusion gives those who have done well in this economy a false sense of entitlement that they have succeeded solely on the basis of individual merit. Conversely, those who have not fared well are viewed as personal failures, derelict in some way. Nothing could be further from the truth. As University of Texas economist James Galbraith notes, "relative wages are much more a matter of politics, and much less a matter of markets than is generally believed." [2]

FROM "BAD" JOBS TO "GOOD" JOBS

The nearest equivalent to the plight of the low-wage worker of today is that of the industrial worker of the thirties. Many of those workers lived outside the mainstream. They too faced a gross imbalance of power. Auto, steel, and other industrial jobs of the thirties paid low wages, had few benefits, and provided dirty and unsafe working conditions. Congress and the courts were generally unsympathetic to these workers' concerns. Most corporations defended the status quo and were especially hostile to efforts by their employees to organize. What ultimately changed these "bad" jobs into "good" jobs was a combination of worker mobilization through unions and a socially conscious, aspiring middle class fighting in the political arena on behalf of these workers.

The period between 1935 and 1945 witnessed the most dramatic changes in labor market institutions in our nation's history. The passage of the National Labor Relations Act in 1935 guaranteed workers the legal right to collectively bargain through a labor union. It specifically made it unlawful for employers to interfere with these worker rights. The results were dramatic. Unionization rates rose from 12 percent of the work-force in 1934 to 35 percent in 1946.[3]

At the height of union representation in the mid-forties, wages rose dramatically and millions of workers were brought into the middle class, creating what would be the most equal distribution of income in the twentieth century.[4] Workers' benefits were also improved through collective bargaining. Union contracts provided health-care coverage, vacation, and pension benefits that were crucial in light of the limited levels of social insurance and medical care provided by the government.[5]

Unions also affected nonunion employers. In the heavily unionized industrial sectors, nonunion employers were forced to raise wages and adopt many of the same benefits of unionized companies in order to stave off unionization and to compete for workers.[6] Implicit competition for workers between industries also spread these union improvements to other sectors of the economy.

Large-scale manufacturers ultimately settled into an arrangement with their workers, sometimes referred to as a "social contract," during this post–World War II period. In contrast to other industrialized countries where benefits and other social welfare provisions were delivered by the government, a private arrangement of employer-provided benefits developed.[7] Workers could generally expect long-term job stability, orderly promotion opportunities, longevity-linked pay, benefit increases, and a promise of a vested pension plan upon retirement.[8] If there were downturns, workers would be laid off, but they would rightfully expect to return to the firm when the economy recovered.

This is not to say that all workers shared in the gains of economic progress. The unionized manufacturing industries were predominantly made up of white males. As a whole, union efforts did not focus on the service sector, except for notable exceptions in the telecommunications and the retail food industries. As a result, this "social contract" did not take root in the service sector or in the small scale, nonunion manufacturing industries. Lower-wage workers, many of whom were women, minorities, and immigrants, were marginalized even in the postwar economic expansion.

Legislatively, unions and their liberal middle-class allies helped enact government programs that aided lower-end workers. Congress passed the Social Security Act in 1935 that gave workers a minimum level of retirement financial security. The first federal minimum wage laws were enacted in 1938 and by 1945 applied to 40 percent of the average hourly manufacturing earnings. Basic protections for laid-off or injured workers and legislation setting a floor on employment standards covering such issues as the maximum hours of work and overtime requirements were put into law. Eventually, legislation of the late sixties and early seventies regulated equal employment opportunity and workplace safety and health. This social safety net and the guarantee of the right to organize and collectively bargain were essential in bringing broadly shared prosperity to workers, establishing norms of behavior, and helping to change industrial jobs into "good" jobs.[9]

A SHIFT IN WORKER POWER

Over the past quarter century, however, a variety of political, economic, and corporate decisions undercut the bargaining power of the average worker, but especially those in the lower strata of the workforce. Those decisions included the push to increase global trade and open global markets, the increase of immigrant workers into the United States, government efforts to deregulate industries that had been highly unionized, Federal Reserve policies that concentrated on reducing the threats of inflation, and a corporate ideological shift that eliminated the postwar social contract with workers and emphasized a principle of maximizing shareholder value. These decisions contributed to the deterioration in low-wage conditions and a worsening of disparities in income and wealth.

Trade with less-developed countries forced American manufacturing workers to compete with workers from low-wage developing countries who earned a fraction of U.S. wages and lacked even minimal legislative protections. Hardest hit were non–native-born, nonwhite workers, workers with less than a college education, and most workers in industries such as textiles, shoes, data input, cars, and steel.[10] And when workers lost their jobs, one in four still were not working after three years and those that got other jobs were generally paid less. These job losses contributed directly to a deterioration in overall wages and increased the number of workers competing for low-wage jobs.[11]

At the same time, the bargaining power of those workers who remained in manufacturing was weakened. The mere threat of foreign competition or relocation led to wage concessions in many manufacturing industries. Buffalo's Trico Products Corporation, purchased by Tomkins PLC in 1998, is one example. Trico, a maker of windshield wipers, began shifting 2,200 jobs to Mexico in the mid-eighties. In the mid-nineties they gave the remaining 300 workers a choice: take a $2.00 an hour cut in pay or the remaining jobs would cross the border.[12] Demands like Trico's lowered pay not just across the auto-parts industries, but also in steel, textiles, shoes, and other tradable goods.[13]

Employers effectively used these same plant closure threats to thwart worker efforts to organize unions.[14] The workers at the Georgia poultry processing plant were threatened that if they voted for the union, the company would close the plant rather than negotiate. Some employers were so blatant as to put moving trucks outside the plant with signs that said *Mexico*.[15] Others attached shipping labels to equipment throughout the plant with a Mexican address or posted maps of North America with an arrow pointing south from the current plant site to Mexico.[16]

After passage of the North American Free Trade Agreement (NAFTA), employer threats to close a plant and move it to thwart organizing activities became more widespread. A study by Cornell economist Kate Bronfenbrenner for the Labor Secretariat of the North American Commission for Labor Cooperation found that employers—regardless of their economic condition—used the threat to close a plant in nearly two-thirds of all organizing campaigns.[17] These threats proved very effective. At the plants where closure was threatened, workers voted for the union in less than a third of the cases in contrast to a 47 percent win rate where no such threats were made.[18]

As our borders opened more broadly to trade, the immigrant

share of the population grew significantly.[19] Between 1970 and 1996, the number of foreign-born increased by fifteen million, increasing from 4.8 percent to 9.3 percent of the U.S. population.[20] While a large share of these new immigrants had more than sixteen years of schooling, a disproportionately high number of immigrants had fewer than nine years, increasing the number of lower-end workers and exerting a downward pressure on wages.[21] Although that effect was diminished in the tight labor market of the late nineties, it still reduced the bargaining power of those already in the market by increasing competition for jobs.[22]

The government's decision to deregulate major industries beginning in the late-seventies also diminished the power of hourly workers. Prior to deregulation, industries such as trucking, railroads, airlines, and telecommunications were heavily unionized: 49 percent of trucking workers, 83 percent of railroad workers, 46 percent of airline workers, and 59 percent of telecommunication workers. With minimal new competition and a large proportion of the industry organized, unions could more easily bargain for better wages and working conditions, resulting in wages that were 14 percent higher than their counterparts in other industries.[23]

After deregulation, worker power in these industries deteriorated. As new nonunion, lower-wage operators entered the market, unionization rates dropped in these industries—in some cases by as much as one-half.[24] This erosion of power led to significantly declining wages. In trucking, for example, real wages declined by 30 percent or four times the average hourly worker wage decline across all industries.[25]

The abandonment of the government's goal to pursue full employment and instead focus on fighting inflation also contributed to the plight of lower-wage workers. From 1945 to 1970, the government focused on ensuring high rates of economic growth, low unemployment, and price stability.[26] In the wake of OPEC-induced energy price hikes and government borrowing in the sixties to pay for the Vietnam War, there was a shift in government policy. Fighting inflation became the number-one governmental priority, and the Federal Reserve became the institution responsible for enforcing that priority.[27]

Adherence to this anti-inflation policy meant that the bargaining power of lower-wage workers was continuously undermined as growth was slowed and unemployment increased. "In periods of high employment," James Galbraith notes, "the weak gain ground on the strong; in periods of high unemployment, the strong gain ground on the weak."[28] Only beginning in the mid-nineties did the Federal Reserve allow unemployment to drop below 5 percent without increasing interest rates.

Technological innovation, especially information and communication technologies, increased demand for workers with certain technical skills.[29] However, lower-wage workers with the least opportunities for employer-sponsored training were generally unable to take advantage of these more technically-skilled jobs. For many of them, technological innovation either eliminated or de-skilled their jobs. The banking industry is a good example. Improvements in technology made it possible for banks to de-skill and relocate back-office work to centralized customer-service operations in large, off-site locations that provide jobs with low wages and few career opportunities.[30]

Finally, the U.S. corporate relationship with its employees changed.[31] In a world of new global and domestic competition, the threat of unfriendly takeovers, restructuring opportunities provided by the new information and telecommunication technologies, and the realignment of executive compensation in the form of stock options, corporations refocused their objectives on increasing shareholder value. To do so, more than one-half of the nations' largest corporations chose to cut costs by firing workers—"downsizing"—in 1991 and 1992. Employers also reduced their short-run labor costs by cutting wages and benefits. They restructured and outsourced jobs. They hired contingent workers and relocated to low-wage regions in the United States and throughout the world. They shifted costs and risks to workers by increasing health insurance premiums and deductibles and substituting pension plans in which the employer ensured workers a certain benefit upon retirement to ones in which benefits were dependent on market returns.[32] And in the end, they saw their corporate responsibility not as balancing the interests of employees, shareholders, and other stakeholders but merely as maximizing shareholder wealth.[33]

UNDER ATTACK:
LOW-WAGE WORKERS GET LITTLE HELP

Many of these economic, political, and corporate policy changes have received attention from academics, researchers, public policy think tanks, and the press. Each policy change diminished the power and well-being of workers in the lower parts of the labor market. Less attention, however, has been given to the fact that during this same period, the most vulnerable workers were deprived of many of the institutions, laws, and political allies that generally helped to counterbalance these forces.[34] Liberal allies who historically had championed their interests mostly sat silent.[35] Unions were in decline. Minimum-wage laws, fair employment laws, and labor laws were all undercut. Government and corporations, instead of working to shore up those institutions that had historically helped these workers and given them power, attacked and weakened them in a way that, according to Université de Montréal economics professors Nicole M. Fortin and Thomas Lemieux, "was unprecedented in recent U.S. labor market history."[36]

The most severely weakened institution over the past thirty years has been the labor movement. The increase in global trade and deregulation of major industries eliminated many unionized jobs in large-scale manufacturing industries. Among the high school graduate workforce, unionization rates fell by almost one half.[37] But unions also played a part in reducing their influence. Instead of aggressively organizing in the expanding service industries during the seventies and eighties, unions turned inward and devoted most of their energies and resources to protecting existing members.[38] The labor movement's weakened political position showed up most glaringly in 1978, when, with both a Democratic president and a Democratic Congress, it was unable to strengthen the labor laws that already had lost much of their ability to protect the workers' rights to organize.

But it was the government's wholesale assault on unions, beginning with President Reagan's firing of the striking air traffic controllers and destruction of its union, that led to the labor movement's precipitous decline. After the conservative victory in the eighties, a disdain for government social policies and an attack on collective bargaining became a key element of the new ideology. Lacking government protection and subjected to employer opposition, private-sector unionization rates plummeted during the eighties, falling from 25 percent of the workforce in 1979 to 16 percent in 1990.[39] Today, less than 11 percent of the private sector labor force is organized.[40] Membership levels now are as low as they were in the early thirties before the enactment of the National Labor Relations Act.[41]

Employers, emboldened by the government's antiunion stance, also took a more combative and adversarial approach in bargaining for pay and benefits with their already unionized workers.[42] Some aggressively tried to get rid of their workers' union through a variety of tactics including relocation abroad or to nonunion communities.[43] Employers also waged virulent antiunion campaigns against worker organizing that Theodore St. Antoine, president of the National Academy of Arbitrators and former dean of the University of Michigan School of Law, describes as having "no parallel in the Western industrialized world." [44] And employers could act with impunity. America's ineffective labor laws provide no disincentive.

The National Labor Relations Act guarantees workers the right to form and join unions for the purpose of collective bargaining. It specifically makes it unlawful for employers to interfere with these worker rights. But saying workers have this right to organize today is like saying African Americans had a right to vote in the Jim Crow South. Surveys dating back to 1970 document that more than 30–45 percent of nonunion workers want to be represented by a union if given the chance. Most workers, however, never are given that opportunity.[45] As MIT management professor Thomas Kochan observes, "Employer resistance to unions is so strong and American labor law is so weak that workers are effectively prohibited from organizing."[46]

As a 2000 Human Rights Watch Report documented, "workers who try to form and join trade unions to bargain with their employers are spied on, harassed, pressured, threatened, suspended, fired, deported, or otherwise victimized in reprisal for their exercise of the right to freedom of association."[47] When an organizing campaign began at Cynthia Porter's Alabama nursing home, her boss called each worker into his office. "He told us that it's important to think the way he thought and we'll get along. I was afraid of what the administrator would do to me. I'd be walking the streets if I lost my job."

When workers are fired for trying to organize a union, the workers, their families, and the organizing efforts suffer. One day in 1996, Bill Fairley's supervisor at his Owensboro, Kentucky, packing plant said he'd heard Fairley had been promoting a union campaign. The next day he was fired. "My wife worked but our income was cut by half. I almost lost my car and my house. I had to pawn my wife's engagement ring. My daughter couldn't go to college. The bill collectors were calling all the time. There was a lot of tension and arguing. You wouldn't think if you lose your job it would domino down and hurt your whole family, but it does." After more than two years, the National Labor Relations Board (NLRB) determined that Bill had been illegally fired for union activities and ordered that he be reinstated. "All the company had to do was give me back pay. Nothing can make up for all the hardship my family had to endure."

These acts of illegal employer intimidation have accelerated in recent years.[48] In 1950 the number of workers who suffered reprisals for trying to organize a union was in the hundreds each year. That number climbed into the thousands, reaching 6,000 in 1969. By 1990, more than 20,000 workers each year were victims of discrimination leading to back-pay orders.[49] Harvard Law School professor Paul Weiler found that unfair labor-practice charges against employers increased by 750 percent between 1957 and 1980.[50] To put it another way, approximately one out of four representation elections result in at least one worker being illegally discharged.[51] As Aaron Bernstein in *Business Week* concluded in 1994, "Over the past dozen years, U.S. industry has conducted one of the most successful antiunion wars ever, illegally firing thousands of workers for exercising their rights to organize."[52]

It is not just the fear of being fired, however, which intimidates workers.[53] Underlying all this employer opposition to their workers' organizing is the raw power employers have over their workers. Employers determine whether a worker can pay the rent and put food on the table for their family. They control their daily lives. They can help workers, harm them, give them favors, discipline or suspend them.[54] They can dismiss them at will for no reason whatsoever. This inherent power gives employers enormous influence over workers pondering whether to support a union.[55]

Employer opposition, however, does not end there. Legal delays by the company can tie up the representation process for years. There is the case of Avondale shipyard in New Orleans, in which the NLRB found that the company violated the workers' rights to organize by transferring union supporters to more difficult and dirtier jobs, by threatening to close the yard if a majority of workers voted for the union, by interrogating and spying on union supporters, by firing twenty-eight union supporters, and by threatening to fire other union supporters. In spite of these flagrant violations of the law, it was not until eight years later that bargaining began, and it occurred only because Avondale was sold to Litton Industries, who agreed to abide by the Board's ruling.[56]

Even if workers finally succeed in obtaining a union, there is little incentive for employers to reach an agreement with the workers. In fact, they are denied a first contract in more than one-third of the cases because the conflicts surrounding the organizing campaign continue into the negotiating process.[57] "Any employer intent on resisting workers' self-organization can drag out legal proceedings for years," Human Rights Watch found, "fearing little more than an order to post a written notice in the workplace promising not to repeat unlawful conduct and grant back pay to a worker fired for organizing." [58]

When one looks at the public sector, where there is minimal employer resistance, the impact of employer opposition becomes apparent. In contrast to the declining unionization rates in the private sector, public-sector organizing soared during the same period. In 1955, 400,000 public workers were union members, but by the early seventies that figure had grown to over four million.[59] Today 37 percent of government employees are union members.[60] Workers in the public sector vote for unions more than 85 percent of the time in contrast to a 50 percent rate in the private sector.[61]

The negative impact of a weak labor movement on lower-wage workers cannot be overstated. Unions have the largest impact on workers in the lower end of the wage spectrum.[62] Unionized high school graduates, for example, earn 21 percent more than the equivalent nonunion workers. They raise the wages of union members in the lowest and second-lowest fifths by 27.9 percent and 16.2 percent, respectively. Some estimate that unions increase wages for these workers by as much as 30 percent. When total compensation is considered, it is much higher.[63]

Unions bring other benefits to these workers. The rate of health-care insurance coverage is up to 35 percent higher in union than in nonunion establishments, with the greatest advantage in smaller establishments.[64] A full 92 percent of full-time employees covered by a collective bargaining agreement in the 1991–1992 period received health-care benefits from their employers.[65] Workers covered by a union contract are more likely to be offered a retirement plan by their employer than nonunion workers, and nearly all the unionized plans are fully funded by employers.[66] Through information and help provided by their unions, union members are also better able to gain access to social protections already in place.[67] For example, union members who were eligible for unemployment insurance benefits were 20 percent more likely to receive those benefits than their nonunion counterparts.[68]

Union decline has other negative effects. Unions bring the

only voice low-wage workers have in their workplace.[69] As Cynthia Porter explains, "You have no input in terms of patient care. They won't listen to you. They tell you, if you don't like it, there's the door. I need to be able to talk to my administrator and have them listen without being afraid of being fired."

Without a strong labor movement, nonunion employers do not have to compete with unionized employers offering better wages and benefits. "In the past, union gains have spilled over to nonunion facilities where management adopted practices that protected workers as a way of buying out some of the interest in unions," Wharton School of Business professor Peter Capelli observes. "But as the threat of union organizing declines, nonunion companies are increasingly abandoning those practices in a kind of reverse spillover." [70]

Historically, the labor movement played a key role in the fight for social legislation beneficial to low-wage workers. They provided a link between the Democratic Party and the working class and pushed the party to address the interests of these workers.[71] With the decline in labor's power, the Democratic Party has focused little on these economic issues, and unions have been less able to secure legislation favorable to low-wage workers.

Liberals, who in the past had fought for the economic interests of vulnerable workers, stayed on the sidelines. Unlike the liberals of the New Deal era who focused on taming the excesses of unbridled capitalism and on broad issues of economic class, liberals of the post-fifties focused more on individual rights and bringing formerly disenfranchised groups into the economic mainstream.[72] While the economic agenda of the New Deal had successfully incorporated white males into the benefits of

American life, it left out women and people of color. Liberals refocused their political agendas to confront rampant race discrimination, eventually challenging discrimination against
women, ethnic minorities, gays and lesbians, and people with
disabilities. These new agendas succeeded in the sixties and seventies and gave legal rights and opportunities to previously excluded groups. But low-wage workers as a group got little
support.[73]

This erosion of political representation precluded these
workers from effectively fighting against the dismantling of
many vital New Deal protections. One of the most important
of these social protections, the minimum wage, was dramatically undercut. During the eighties, its value plummeted by
more than 30 percent. Despite legislative increases in 1990 and
1991 and again in 1996 and 1997, the value of the minimum
wage in 1999 was still 21 percent less than in 1979.[74] The relative minimum wage averaged around 50 percent of the average
hourly wages in manufacturing throughout the sixties, but by
the nineties it had fallen to around 30 percent.[75] Even *Business
Week* called for a hike in the minimum wage in 2000, noting
that the percentage of full-time workers living in poverty was
no lower than it was in 1994.[76]

Because the minimum wage acts as a reference point for employers in determining a starting wage and the wage structure
around it, its decline affects not only those below the minimum
wage but also those near it.[77] Government's failure to keep the
minimum wage at its 1968 levels affected nearly one-fifth of
the workforce.[78] Women, who make up nearly 60 percent of
the minimum-wage workforce and nearly three-quarters of the

low-wage workforce, were the hardest hit, seeing a precipitous decline in their wages.[79]

Other employment and labor laws were also undercut, which left low-wage workers with few protections—unemployment insurance being one of the most important. Between 1950 and 1980, about one-half of the unemployed received unemployment (UI) benefits. By the mid-eighties, because of program changes that tightened eligibility requirements, only a third received benefits.[80] Most of those not covered were lower-wage workers who did not meet the minimum hours and earnings requirements that most states impose for eligibility.[81] In 1995, more than twice the number of higher-wage workers received benefits than lower-wage workers, even though low-wage workers suffer twice the unemployment rate.[82] The effects of this lack of coverage were visible in the first economic downturn of this new century, in which low-wage workers disproportionately bore the brunt of the decline in lost jobs and reduced hours.

Low-wage workers who are laid off have little ability to cope during the transition to a new job without unemployment insurance. They have few, if any, resources to help them. As a recent government report noted:

> . . . as a safety net, the UI program continues to offer only minimal protection for low-wage workers. Even though employers in many states pay the same UI payroll taxes for employees earning minimum wage as they pay for employees earning far more than that amount, low-wage workers are much less likely than higher-wage workers to be included in the UI safety net.[83]

At the same time, the federal government slashed budgets of many agencies in charge of employee protections, leaving them powerless to enforce the acts. The Occupational Safety and Health Administration (OSHA) is a glaring example. Since its creation in 1971, OSHA had been suffering from underfunding and understaffing. But starting in the Reagan years, the number of inspectors was reduced by an additional 20 percent.[84] Low-wage workers, who work in the most unsafe and unhealthy workplaces, were the most directly affected. Without any representation in the workplace and little government oversight, workers suffered the consequences. In the poultry processing industry, where most workers are immigrants with limited knowledge of their rights, workers face injury rates twice that of the national average for manufacturing. Meat-packing plants had the highest incidence of injury and illness of any industry in 1999.[85] Unless there is government oversight, there is little chance that these conditions will improve.

It is no accident, then, that in the midst of the economic changes of the past three decades, America's poorest workers fared worse than those in other industrialized countries.[86] "Trade unions, wage-setting power, a strong minimum wage and social legislation are crucial in bringing power and improvement to lower-wage workers," Harvard economists Richard Freeman and Lawrence Katz point out.[87] It is the lack of strong labor market institutions in the United States, as compared to the rest of the industrialized world, that accounts for this difference in outcomes.[88]

CHALLENGING THE POWER IMBALANCE: A BEGINNING

An emerging broad-based movement is beginning to articulate a different vision of America: a society that measures success not by the ups and downs of the stock market but instead by the well-being of working families. Groups and individuals are working at the state and local levels with low-wage workers to improve their lives. Revitalized labor unions and a reinvigorated AFL-CIO are playing their part in this new activism.

The Service Employees International Union (SEIU) health-care campaign in California is a telling example of how unions are improving the quality of today's lower-wage jobs. SEIU, in collaboration with disability and senior citizens groups, pressured counties throughout California to engage in collective bargaining with its home health-care workers after it helped to enact legislation that gave these counties collective bargaining authority. The SEIU then went door-to-door to sign up workers—with success that has been nothing short of astounding. Out of the approximately 200,000 home care workers in the State of California In-Home Supportive Services system, the SEIU today represents about 130,000 of these workers—75,000 in Los Angeles alone.

As a result of the organizing campaign, home care workers in the Bay area, who in 1995 made $4.25 an hour with few if any benefits, make $10.00 an hour. They have employer-provided medical, dental, and vision coverage, and paid time off through a vacation fund. The union also helps match workers with potential clients and provides needed transportation.

A strong union presence in the hotel industry is changing formerly low-paid, no-benefit jobs into good jobs. Maria Sanchez, a Las Vegas guest-room attendant at a casino hotel, can now support her family. She earns $10.50 an hour, with employer-provided health benefits, sick leave, and a pension. Sanchez can be retrained for free at the Culinary Training Academy and qualify for higher-paying positions within the industry. In Reno, Nevada, a town with a comparable living standard, her counterpart earns only $7.48 an hour with few benefits. The only difference between the two employees is that Maria is represented by the Culinary Workers Union and the Reno worker is not. In Las Vegas over 40,000 hotel workers are represented by a union and almost one-third of the industry is organized. Guest-room attendants, baggage porters, front-desk clerks, and cooks earn an average of 40 percent more than workers in identical occupations in Reno. There, less than 2 percent of the hotel industry is unionized.[89]

The ability to dominate a labor market has produced substantial gains for janitors. In the past ten years, the SEIU's Justice for Janitors Campaign has organized over 75,000 janitors.[90] In northern New Jersey, for example, janitors moved from $5.50 to $11.00 an hour over the three-year life of the contract and are now provided health insurance. Just as important, part-time jobs have been changed to full-time, giving workers needed hours. Certainly, not all the gains have been that dramatic, but they have been substantial.[91]

To ensure that unionized janitorial contractors are not at a competitive disadvantage, the union attempts to organize an entire labor market in a city or region. When this is achieved, janitorial employers cannot use low wages as a tool for winning contracts from building owners. Because many of the real estate owners and building-service contractors have a nationwide scope, the union uses the power of its membership in one area to help organize another. Janitorial jobs that largely were poorly paid and lacking benefits have been changed for the better through this approach.

The labor movement is also moving beyond traditional forms of representation in order to respond directly to the needs of low-wage workers. One of the most exciting examples of these new strategies is the South Bay Central Labor Council in San Jose, California. In partnership with community groups, it created Working Partnerships USA, an organization with the purpose of bringing a wider range of voices to the table in discussions about regional economic development and state and national employment policy. Through grassroots campaigns, research, education, and a broad community planning process, Working Partnerships USA is changing the terms of the debate, attempting to ensure that the social and economic well-being of community residents be the central concern in strategies for economic development of Silicon Valley. One of the results was the passage of San Jose's living-wage ordinance.

To respond to the needs of temporary workers, Working Partnerships USA developed Together @ Work, a worker-owned temporary agency whose aim is to give voice to the growing number of temporary and contingent workers with limited access to living wages, health care, pensions, and career development. The organization pays workers a higher wage than competing temp agencies and takes a smaller employer commission.

At the same time, it provides training and benefits for its members, which allows them to qualify for better paying jobs.

Unions, women's and civil rights groups, immigrant organizations, worker and community advocacy groups such as ACORN and Jobs with Justice, religious groups, students, and caring Americans are working in coalitions to enact living-wage ordinances that require businesses that qualify for public monies to pay a living wage. There are now more than seventy-five living-wage ordinances across the country in cities such as St. Louis, Boston, Los Angeles, Tucson, San Jose, Portland, Milwaukee, Detroit, Minneapolis, and Oakland.[92]

These coalitions have been successful because they speak a powerful truth: working Americans are entitled to a living wage. They work because they brought a wide range of community members into the planning process and combined this grassroots knowledge with critical strategic analysis. And they are successful because they provide the leverage to convince politicians to stand up for workers.

Many of the living-wage coalition partners are also playing a central role in other local initiatives to improve the lives of the working poor. Through its Project Quest in San Antonio, the Industrial Areas Foundation—a national network of forty organizations—trains workers from low-income communities and teams them up with employers who have a commitment to provide quality jobs with mobility. Omaha-based Appleseed has pursued legal and community-based strategies to improve the lives of meat processing and packing workers by getting commitments from employers to abide by codes of conduct.

To help workers in nonstandard jobs, Working Today, a national membership organization based in New York, provides workers access to group rates for health insurance, prepaid legal advice and pensions, and works with its members to further their interests in the political arena. Immigrant workers have been helped by the Workplace Project's Long Island–based immigrant workers' center. The center spearheaded legislation to strengthen the penalties against employers who were paying immigrant workers below the minimum wage.

Women's groups have provided leadership on work and family issues. The National Partnership for Women and Families, in concert with a myriad of women's, labor, and child advocate groups, was instrumental in helping to pass the Family and Medical Leave Act. They are once again leading the political fight for paid family leave, a change especially important to workers in low-wage jobs. They testified on behalf of labor-law reform to ensure the right to organize, understanding that unions have a profound effect on improving the lives of women workers. Poverty and low-wage jobs are women's issues.

Family and child advocates understand the inextricable link between the hardships faced by the working poor and the devastating impact on their children. The Children's Defense Fund continues to advocate for improvements for low-wage workers. Families USA and other family advocates are fighting hard to ensure that working Americans and their families have access to affordable health care. Dozens of family and child advocacy groups are working to enact legislation to address child care, early education, and health-care policies.

The religious community is playing an important role in bringing a moral and spiritual dimension to the fight against

worker injustice. Baltimoreans United in Leadership Development (BUILD), composed of essentially black church congrega-
tions, together with the American Federation of State, County,
and Municipal Employees (AFSCME) and other community
groups, spearheaded passage of the Baltimore living-wage ordinance in 1994, the first in the country. That ordinance raised the
wages of 4,000 employees of Baltimore city service contractors
from $4.24 to $6.10 an hour.

The National Interfaith Committee for Worker Justice edu-
cates, organizes, and mobilizes the American religious community on issues and campaigns that improve the wages, benefits,
and working conditions of low-wage workers in nursing homes,
hotels, restaurants, poultry plants, and in facilities operated by
religious institutions. They encourage religious participation in
living-wage campaigns and coordinate programs between
workers, people of faith, unions, farmers, and environmentalists
to promote workers' rights.

Students are also fighting against worker injustice. Through
United Students Against Sweatshops, students have helped to
fight against overseas sweatshops. Students at the nine-campus
University of California system pressured the university administration to sign a comprehensive anti-sweatshop code, requiring
companies licensed to create materials with school logos to pay a
living wage, comply with environmental and health and safety
laws, and eliminate any employee discrimination based on preg-
nancy or union organizing. When companies fail to adhere to
these standards, students have engaged in boycotts of their products and have pushed hard for an independent monitoring system to ensure compliance.[92]

Student efforts have also focused on improving the jobs of low-wage workers on their own campuses by staging sit-ins and demonstrations to require a living wage, fair benefits, a safe workplace, and freedom of association and collective bargaining. One of the first university living-wage campaigns was at Johns Hopkins University in spring 2000. Campaigns made up of coalitions of students, workers, faculty, and concerned community members have also been waged at other schools, including the University of Virginia, Brown, Wesleyan, University of Tennessee-Knoxville, and Harvard.

Consumer groups are playing their part. The Consumers Union has been active in trying to improve health-care access. The Consumer Federation of America has worked in coalitions to improve workers' wages. In the Care for the Caregivers Alabama Campaign against Beverly Enterprises—one of the largest nursing home chains in the country—workers joined with elderly and consumer groups. As a result of this campaign, led by the United Food and Commercial Workers Union, workers received a $2.00 per hour raise, health-care benefits, and greater worker involvement in patient care.

Some companies are also playing a role. Firms who want to treat their workers fairly are at a competitive disadvantage. In health care, they are actually subsidizing employers who refuse to provide coverage to their own employees. Recently the Chamber of Commerce and the Business Roundtable joined with unions, health-insurance organizations, and family organizations to call for health coverage for the uninsured. Companies are also working with labor and immigrant rights groups, such as the National Immigration Forum, to reform America's immigration laws and eliminate what even Daniel T. Griswold of the conservative Cato Institute calls, a "black market in labor, with all the pathologies of smuggling, fraudulent documents, wage distortions, inefficiencies, and abuses that attend it." [93]

Corporations for Social Responsibility has been an active force in broadening the role of corporations to include responsibility to workers, communities, and the environment. Even CEOs in the Business Roundtable have moved beyond their stated belief that rewarding shareholders is a corporation's only function to at least a tacit acceptance that corporations have some responsibility to workers and their communities. Recently they also supported a tax cut for lower-income Americans including a one-year moratorium on payroll taxes.

·   ·   ·

Coalitions of concerned Americans can make a difference in the lives of the working poor. To end the exploitation of working Americans, these coalitions and efforts must expand. Worker injustice affects us all. It is a civil rights issue, a student issue, a family issue, an environmental justice issue, an immigrant issue, a consumer issue, a religious issue, a business issue. Ultimately, it is a human rights issue.

While these recent efforts have helped some workers, more is needed. The well-being of hard-working Americans and their families should not be left to chance. We must, as a society, set new ground rules for work in the twenty-first century. Workers must be assured that their work provides the basic necessities for a decent life for themselves and their families.

CHAPTER 8

A Compact with Working Americans

This society needs to agree on a new set of principles—a compact with working Americans—that establishes the obligations and responsibilities of employers and government to workers. This compact has a simple and clear purpose: workers should be assured that if they work hard they will be treated fairly and have the resources to provide for themselves and their families.

Certainly, there will be disagreements on how best to provide these supports and implement these goals. We must take into account that America's economy has changed in the last three decades. Workers are more mobile. The average job tenure is three years. Women are now a much larger segment of the workforce than ever before. Yet, we cannot get so bogged down in the how-tos that we lose sight of Flor Segunda, Cynthia Porter, Bob Butler, and Linda Stevens, who are struggling to survive every day. Failing to respond is unacceptable. Now is the time to face this harsh injustice. We have the power to change these conditions.

A COMPACT WITH WORKING AMERICANS
AMERICANS WHO WORK SHOULD BE ASSURED:

- Sufficient Income to Meet A Family's Basic Needs
- Affordable Health Care
- Flexibility and Support to Properly Care for One's Family
- Opportunities to Gain New Skills
- Affordable and Safe Housing
- A Safe and Healthy Work Environment
- Security in Time of Economic Adversity and Retirement
- The Right to Organize and Collectively Bargain
- Fair Trade and Immigration Policies

WORKERS MUST BE ASSURED SUFFICIENT INCOME TO MEET A FAMILY'S BASIC NEEDS

RAISE THE MINIMUM WAGE AND INDEX IT

The minimum wage must be raised to the "official" poverty line and indexed. This increase can be accomplished in two steps. Government inaction over the past generation has meant a nearly $2.00 cut in the real value of the minimum wage. Today the real value of the minimum wage is 30 percent lower than its peak value, which was in 1968.[1] It must be immediately brought up to $7.09 per hour, which is what the current value would be if it had been allowed to keep up with inflation. But more must be done. We must also give these workers a raise, and at the very least the minimum wage should be increased to the "official" poverty line. For a family of four this means an annual income of $18,100, or $8.70 an hour for a full-time worker, still well below—in many cases less than half—what it actually takes a family of four to meet their daily needs. This raise would begin to address the long fall of pretax income for lower-end workers in the midst of rising productivity and profits over the past two decades.[2]

Equally important, the minimum wage should be automatically indexed.[3] Increases should not be used as a political football while the most vulnerable workers fall further behind. States with higher costs of living should be encouraged to raise their state minimum wages above the federal level to reflect those costs. Ten states and the District of Columbia already have minimum wages above the federal minimum standard.

Some argue that the minimum wage is not an appropriate mechanism to help these workers because it is poorly targeted. They contend that increases will not go to the lower-income adults who are the intended recipients. These critics are simply wrong. Almost 60 percent of the benefits from an increase would go to families with working, prime-aged adults in the bottom 40 percent of the income distribution, one-third of whom have children.[4] In fact, nearly 4.7 million children depend at least in part on the earnings of a minimum wage–earning parent.[5] Women, who represent 60 percent of minimum wage workers, would certainly benefit, as would minorities.

Raising the income of low-income working families is not the only purpose of the minimum wage. Wages below a certain level are contrary to societal values, regardless of the economic condition of the worker. It provides an important floor on wages at the low end of the labor market.[6]

Finally, there is the argument that increasing the minimum wage would hurt the very ones that it is intended to help by increasing unemployment at the low end. But recent studies show that the proposed increases would have a minimal unemployment effect.[7]

A GOAL OF FULL EMPLOYMENT

One of the least appreciated policies to lift the bargaining power of lower-wage workers and improve their jobs is full employment.[8] In contrast to the eighties and early nineties, when unemployment rates hit 6 percent and lower-end workers' wages declined, 1995–2000 saw record low unemployment, which increased the bargaining power of low-wage workers and improved their wages for the first time in decades.[9] Low unemployment forces employers to bid up wages at the low end. As unemployment now returns to higher levels, the lower end of the labor market once again is being hardest hit in increased layoffs and reduction of hours and wages. If we are serious about improving low-wage jobs, our monetary and fiscal policy should emphasize full employment.

BUSINESSES THAT RECEIVE PUBLIC MONIES SHOULD PROVIDE QUALITY JOBS

Government distributes billions of dollars to businesses through government contracts, subsidies, and tax assistance every year. If businesses choose to benefit from these public monies, they should be required to provide quality jobs. Public dollars should reflect public values and provide a public service, not enrich corporate executives and shareholders or subsidize poverty-level, dead-end jobs.

In the nursing home industry, where 85 percent of nursing home revenues come from federal and state largesse in the form of Medicaid and Medicare, quality of care would improve if companies were required to provide quality jobs in return for public funding.[10] At the same time, taxpayers would be spared the hidden costs of subsidizing poor workers through Medicaid, food stamps, and other government programs.

Living-wage ordinances require recipients of public monies to pay a living wage. The ordinances cover employers who hold large city or county service contracts or receive substantial public financial assistance in the form of grants, loans, bond financing, or other economic development subsidies. These subsidies can take the form of tax abatements, below-market provisions of city services, or new infrastructures to facilitate a factory or office building.

Most ordinances use the official poverty level for a family of four to determine a living wage. San Jose's 1998 living-wage ordinance requires service contractors to pay $9.50 an hour with health benefits or $10.75 without, thus taking into account San Jose's higher cost of living. More than one-half of the ordinances have a cost-of-living adjustment, and many go beyond wages and require other job quality standards.[11] In San Jose, a company's labor practices are taken into consideration and successor contractors must offer jobs to employees of predecessor contractors who performed those services as a condition of receiving any public monies.[12] In Minneapolis, preferential treatment is given to firms that engage in "responsible labor relations."

Some economists contend that these policies are self-defeating because increasing the pay for some workers above market levels will reduce the overall employment of low-wage workers. But a recent study by a longtime critic of the minimum wage, David Neumark of Michigan State University, finds such fears exaggerated. Analyzing the living-wage experience of thirty-six cities, he found that, on balance, the higher wages brought about by living-wage laws appear to outweigh the effect of job losses.[13] And the Economic Policy Institute found no significant increase in costs to the city.[14]

States have also moved to ensure that the millions of dollars in economic development monies serve the broader public interest.[15] In 1995, Minnesota launched the nation's first successful state effort for a subsidy disclosure program. It required that the public be notified and given a chance to comment on proposed subsidies larger than $100,000 from a city and more than $500,000 from the state. The final decision on whether to give a subsidy to a company would be made by an elected public body. Corporate subsidies—including grants, loans, and tax breaks—would have a clearly defined public interest. And state and local government agencies would create standards for all subsidies, including requirements on wages for new jobs.[16] If corporations fail to live up to the agreed-upon standards, they can be fined by the state or forced to pay back the subsidy.

At least thirty-seven states now have standards attached to at least one of their incentive programs, from property tax abatements and training grants to enterprise zones and industrial de-

velopment bonds. Kansas is among the states that have imple-
mented job quality standards. The High Performance Incentive
Program (HPIP) provides incentives to qualified for-profit companies that pay higher than average wages and invest at least 2
percent of their total payroll costs in employee training or participate in workforce training programs.[17]

Control of public financing is a potentially powerful instru-
ment to improve the quality of lower-paid jobs and to set new
standards for how workers are treated. To effectively serve this
purpose, there must be full public disclosure of these contracts,
subsidies, or tax advantages, quality job standards tied to the receipt of these monies, and workable mechanisms of accountability.

STRENGTHEN THE EARNED INCOME TAX CREDIT AND CHILD TAX CREDIT

The Earned Income Tax Credit (EITC), whose early supporters
included Ronald Reagan, is one of the most successful programs
for the working poor and an effective complement to raising the
minimum wage.[18] Enacted in 1975, this refundable tax credit
was designed to offset the regressive effects of Social Security
and Medicare payroll taxes on working-poor families and to
supplement the income of low- and moderate-income working
families.[19] Even with the EITC, those slightly above the poverty
level end up paying high marginal tax rates because the EITC
and other programs phase out.[20] Unlike the minimum wage,
which goes to all workers, the EITC focuses primarily on lower-
income working families with children. As economists Barry
Bluestone of Northeastern University and Teresa Ghilarducci of

Notre Dame point out, it is also "a form of wage insurance" for all working families who temporarily fall on hard times.[21] This is especially important in today's turbulent economy with its increased job instability.[22]

The EITC lifts more children out of poverty than any other government program or category of programs.[23] In 1998 alone, the EITC moved five million people above the poverty line, one-half of whom were children.[24] The maximum dollar amounts go to families who earn between $6,500 and $11,930 with one child and $9,140 and $11,930 with two. The benefits then phase down after $11,930.[25] About 19.7 million workers claimed the EITC in tax year 1998 and received an average credit of $1,547.[26]

Regressive sales, excise, and property taxes at the state and local level still burden the working poor. In 1995 the poorest fifth of married non-elderly families paid an average 12.5 percent of their income for state and local taxes. By contrast, the average burden on the wealthiest 1 percent was 7.9 percent.[27] One way of offsetting these regressive state taxes is the passage of state EITCs to piggyback the federal EITC. Fifteen states and one county have enacted an earned-income tax credit.

At the federal level, the EITC has been helpful in offsetting the rising payroll tax liabilities for those below the poverty level. Yet improvements are needed. Several reforms should be considered, including raising the income level at which EITC benefits phase out, raising the benefit levels, and eliminating the marriage penalty. At the same time, tax policies should be critically examined to ensure that lower-end workers do not shoulder a disproportionate burden.

The Child Tax Credit recognizes the importance and extra costs of child rearing, providing a kind of family allowance for families with children under seventeen. Families receive a credit of $600 per child, and it is scheduled to rise to $700 in 2005, $800 in 2009, and $1,000 in 2010. Because the tax credit can only be used by those wage earners who owe federal income taxes, families not earning enough income receive no child support. The law was changed for 2001 to allow low-income families to claim a part of this "credit." While this was a success in beginning to end the discrimination in subsidies, it did not go far enough. The Child Tax Credit should be made fully refundable so that workers who need the help the most get at least what other families are provided.[28]

ELIMINATE PAY INEQUITIES

Employers can refuse to provide the same pay to part-time workers with the same job as full-time workers. They can also exclude part-time workers from their employer-provided benefits. Employers rationalize this discriminatory practice by arguing that so-called "part-time" jobs are peripheral to an employer's workforce. Yet individuals who work twenty-five hours a week are just as attached to their employer as those who work forty hours a week. Women, who make up 70 percent of the part-time workforce, should not be penalized for working less than full-time schedules. A majority do so to care for their families.

Employers should be prohibited from discriminating against part-time workers, who should receive wage and benefit parity with their full-time counterparts. In the provision of health insurance and pensions—where employee contributions are gen-

erally required—it is unfair to expect part-time workers who
have less take-home pay to make a greater contribution than
full-time workers. A way should be found to either subsidize
these workers or prohibit employers from requiring greater contributions from part-timers. Social entitlements such as Social
Security, pensions, and health insurance must also be redesigned
to be more equitable for part-time workers.

WORKERS SHOULD BE ASSURED AFFORDABLE HEALTHCARE

More than forty million Americans have no health coverage.
More than half are workers who live in households with incomes below 200 percent of poverty.[29] In every year since 1991,
at least 14 percent of the population (including the elderly) has
lacked health insurance for at least a full year.[30] And the number
of uninsured is increasing as health coverage premiums rise and
worker earnings remain stagnant.[31]

There is government-provided health insurance for many
Americans through such programs as Medicare, Medicaid, and
SCHIP: the elderly, many of the destitute, lower-income children, and individuals moving off welfare to work. Middle- and
upper-income Americans receive health subsidies by the exclu-
sion of their employer's health-insurance contributions from
their taxes, by allowing individual tax deductions, and by allowing flexible spending and personal medical funds to reduce tax-
able income. In fact, two-thirds of the $140 billion in annual
health-care tax subsidies go to middle- and upper-income
Americans. Equity dictates that we ensure access to affordable

health-care coverage to lower-income working Americans and their families.

It is long past time to remedy this problem. One straightforward solution to ensure coverage for lower-wage Americans would be to mandate that every employer provide basic health insurance to their workers. One hundred and fifty-eight million Americans and their dependents today receive health insurance through their employers. Employers of low-wage workers frequently fail to provide coverage. Requiring those employers to do so is only fair. Employers who are providing their workers' health insurance should not have to subsidize those who do not. Within this structure we should ensure a seamless system so that someone who loses or changes jobs does not lose coverage.

Another approach would be to extend Medicaid and SCHIP, health-care programs that are now available to most low-income children, to their parents, and other low-income adults. This would not only give needed access to low-income working parents, but it would also increase the number of enrolled children. To further maximize enrollment, states should eliminate bureaucratic hurdles and move to a more "presumptive eligibility" approach similar to the Medicare program.

Under such a plan, all working Americans who meet the income specifications—regardless of their full-time or part-time status—would qualify. And workers who have lost their jobs would continue their coverage while they are in the process of finding another job. If workers are offered an employer health insurance plan, the cost to provide coverage under SCHIP or Medicaid could be used to subsidize the employee or family's health insurance contribution to that employer plan. Workers

would be given the option of going into the SCHIP or Medicaid
plan or into their employer's plan.

WORKERS SHOULD BE ASSURED THE NEEDED
FLEXIBILITY AND SUPPORTS TO PROMOTE
HEALTHY FAMILIES

INCREASED JOB FLEXIBILITY

Workers should not face punishment or loss of financial resources as the price of responding to a family member's basic
needs. For higher-wage workers, it is taken for granted that if
there is a call from school or if their child is sick or a parent
needs help that they can respond without losing a day's pay. This
benefit should not be based on income. A reasonable number of
paid leave days must be established to be used for an employee or
family member's illness, a child's educational or school need or
doctor's appointment, child-care difficulties, or some other family or personal crisis.[32] For workers who already have employer-
provided sick leave, that leave should be allowed for a family
member's illness.[33] Lastly, the United States stands alone in the
industrialized world in not requiring companies to provide paid
vacation time. There must be a minimum paid vacation for all
workers.

Worktime must also be restructured to allow workers the
flexibility to care for their families. The United States has the
longest annual average hours of work in the industrialized
world.[34] We have a 1950s workplace for a twenty-first century

workforce. Women, who are primarily responsible for caregiving, are forced to work in part-time, lower paying jobs.[35]

Employers should provide more flexible schedules and mandatory overtime should be prohibited. In many European countries, companies are experimenting with a variety of ways to restructure their workplaces to allow workers more flexibility, including working-time accounts at some German, Dutch, and Italian firms that provide employees with regularly scheduled time off.[36] In the United States, Congress enacted the Federal Part-Time Career Employment Act of 1978, which made reduced time options available to all federal employees while guaranteeing their continued access to promotional opportunities, proportional salaries, and prorated benefits. This program is an excellent example of the kind of flexibility that is necessary to allow workers who also have caregiving responsibilities to qualify for these jobs.

Basic Supports for Working Families
Paid Family and Medical Leave

The United States stands virtually alone among industrialized countries in having no national program that provides paid family leave.[37] And low-wage workers are the least likely to be provided paid leave by their employers. So most lower-wage workers face the same horrible choice as the Newark janitor Flor Segunda: stay home and face financial hardship or go back to work and miss the first weeks of her child's life.

The Family and Medical Leave Act (FMLA) must be

amended to provide paid leave. Most industrial countries provide at least one year of paid leave. In a recent survey, 80 percent of Americans support "paid parental leave that allows working parents of very young babies to stay home from work to care for their children." [38] It is good public policy. Paid family leave increases women's employment tenure and earnings. [39] And because working women now supply an ever-increasing percent of their families' household income, paid maternity leave is critical. [40] It also provides needed bonding time for parents and newborns.

The FMLA excludes more than half of employed fathers and 60 percent of employed mothers. The Act should be amended to include businesses with fifteen or more employees, eliminate the 1,250-hour requirement of eligibility, and reduce the one-year job tenure requirement to six months. These changes would help low-wage workers, who disproportionately work for smaller employers, work part-time, and have less job stability. At the same time, we should recognize that twelve weeks of family leave does not fully respond to the needs of parents with young children. During the first year of a child's life, new parents need extra time with their children. Workplaces must reflect this parental need. At the end of the twelve-week leave, some form of partial family leave in which workers could have a reduced schedule for a three-month period and receive full pay should be examined.

Most industrial countries provide at least one year of paid leave that is funded in a variety of ways. What is important is that we act to provide paid leave so that parents will not have to face the unconscionable choice between leaving their newborn child or supplying their critical financial needs.

Child Care/Early Education

Nearly three-fourths of mothers with children under eighteen now work outside the home.[41] Each individual family is left to provide for care. This creates a two-tier system in which the well-off can pay for quality child care and low-wage workers cannot. In many states, the cost of child care is twice that of public higher education.

The United States is again alone among industrialized nations in failing to provide broad public child-care assistance.[42] It must move toward a comprehensive system in which all children receive quality child care.[43] A variety of approaches have been suggested.[44] Most provide a baseline subsidy that more accurately reflects the cost of child care. The subsidy goes to all families based on a sliding scale with the largest subsidy going to the poorest families.

Access to child care during nonstandard hours must also be provided. Today, low-wage workers disproportionately work nonstandard hours that few child-care centers serve.[45] Moreover, to improve child-care quality, minimum standards should be developed and vouchers tied to the providers that meet these standards. But quality of care will not improve without improvement in the wages and benefits of child-care workers. Child-care workers are paid less than many workers in fast food restaurants, and their turnover rates reflect this poor treatment. Yet consistency is essential to quality child care and early education. Congress understood this connection when it required in the Military Child Care Act that the rates of pay for child-care workers be equivalent to other employees at the same installation with comparable training, seniority, and experience. With this provision, annual staff turnover dropped from 300 percent to less than 30 percent.[46]

Today, middle- and higher-income Americans receive over $2 billion in government subsidies for child care in the form of federal tax breaks under the Dependent Care Tax Credit (DCTC).[47] The DCTC provides $1,400 per year to a family with two children, regardless of income, which will increase to $2,100 in 2003. Forty-five percent of the DCTC goes to families with adjusted gross incomes of more than $50,000. Because the credit is not refundable, it provides no benefit to those who earn too little to take advantage of it, less than about $25,000 a year for a family of four.[48] In 1998, families in the bottom fifth received just 8 percent of the $2.5 billion in DCTC tax assistance, while families in the top fifth received 21 percent. Higher-income workers also receive government subsidies in the form of pretax accounts for child-care expenses. One way to provide assistance to all parents would be to make the DCTC refundable and to raise the maximum child-care benefit to reflect its true cost. Families earning less than 200 percent of poverty would receive the maximum amount, and those above that level would receive a scaled-down amount based on income. Ten states now have refundable dependent-care tax credits.

In the short term, a simple and modest goal would be to fund child care for all eligible children under the Child Care and Development Fund, a block grant to states that supplies subsidies to lower-income children. Today, only 10 percent of the over ten million eligible children receive assistance.[49] The DCTC eligibility requirements could be capped at $60,000 to help finance these subsidies. The one billion dollar savings could be used to offset the costs of providing more help to low-income children.

Providing these subsidies for all qualified children is simple fairness. It is also a good investment. Quality child care provides a means for lower-income parents to increase their working hours and income. In the most successful programs, social benefits that could be monetized greatly exceeded program costs, with net savings to the government of from $13,000 to $19,000 per child, according to a RAND study.[50] And it is good for business. As workers have more stable quality child-care arrangements, their absenteeism and turnover decreases.

At the age of three, children should be provided universal preschool. This is not a radical idea. Three- and four-year-olds in France and Italy attend publicly funded preschools. The states of Georgia and Oklahoma provide universal preschool for all four-year-olds.[51] And three-quarters of families with incomes over $50,000 a year have children in preschool. Working-poor families with earnings between $10,000 and $35,000 have the lowest rates of enrollment.[52] The children who need help the most are getting the least.[53]

Before- and after-school programs must be provided for school-age children. Nearly seven million children are left home alone each day. The average cost of before- and after-school care is $3,000 per year per child. We must publicly finance these programs either through extension of school days or through need-based vouchers.

And finally, higher education needs to be made affordable for the children of lower-wage workers. Cost barriers to higher education condemn the children of the working poor to the same economic plight as their parents. Other countries assure that the best schools are affordable to students who demonstrate merit, regardless of their parents' income. We cannot proclaim to be for equal opportunity and at the same time effectively preclude these children from getting a college education.

WORKERS SHOULD BE ASSURED THE OPPORTUNITY TO GAIN NEW SKILLS

All workers should be able to get the necessary training to qualify for better-paying jobs. This is particularly true for low-wage workers, who are half as likely to receive employer-provided training or education subsidies as higher-end workers. Yet as I have explained earlier, training alone will not alleviate the problems of low-wage work in America because there are not millions of higher-paying jobs waiting for these newly trained workers. In fact, low-wage occupations will see the greatest increase in numbers among all occupations. But for certain low-wage workers, training will lead to better jobs if the training is linked to job opportunities requiring these newfound skills. Such opportunities will occur most effectively where there is a system of job ladders or internal labor markets to provide the next level of employment.

A variety of strategies have emerged in recent years, not only providing employers with well-trained workers, but also improving the quality of the jobs and creating career paths. Unlike many traditional training programs that resulted in minimal economic improvements—in large part owing to the lack of connection between local employers and the training—these strategies tightly link training to particular occupational or industrial markets.[54]

Union and employer partnerships dominate this area. Unions have the ability to bring a wide variety of employers together, and because they understand the nature of competition in an industry, they can effectively pool resources from a variety of sources. And there are good jobs available under the collective bargaining agreement for those workers who have completed training. At the national level, Working for America works with local union leaders to build these cross-employer, industry-specific partnerships.

The Philadelphia employment-training initiative, a joint project of the National Union of Hospital and Health Care Employees, American Federation of State, County, and Municipal Employees, and District 1199C—the city's largest health-care local—is such an example. Today, sixty-one employers contribute to the fund, which serves an estimated 10,000 people per year. The Fund's Breslin Learning Center is housed in center city Philadelphia and is open fourteen hours a day, seven days a week to all Philadelphia residents. At the Learning Center, students are placed into training based on an academic assessment and career counseling. A wide range of remedial coursework is available, including job readiness, literacy, and English for speakers of other languages. No one is turned away based on academic need. In its nurse-training program, the union helps trainees advance from certified nursing assistant to licensed practical nurse and then to registered nurse. Most of their trainees are minorities who have traditionally had little access to highly skilled nursing positions.[55]

The Culinary Workers Union Local 226, through its Culinary Training Academy in Las Vegas, provides the means for workers to move into better jobs in the hotel industry. The Academy trainees—a third of whom earn less than $10,000 a year—receive tuition-free training in the broad range of occupations covered under the local's contract. These occupations range from housekeeping and kitchen positions to food and beverage service. Seventy percent of its graduates find jobs at union-represented hotels, with excellent benefits and wages starting at $10.70 an hour. Retention for graduates placed in union jobs is twice that for workers without training from the Academy. Participants have the opportunity to return for training to upgrade their skills and advance their careers.[56]

This same concept has been successful in Milwaukee's manufacturing industry. In the late nineties, retirements in the city's older workforce and a low jobless rate created a shortage of skilled manufacturing workers. The movement of firms from the inner city, where many workers live, to the suburbs complicated the problem of meeting the manufacturing employers' workforce needs. The Wisconsin Regional Training Partnership (WRTP), founded in 1992 and jointly governed by business, labor, and public-sector representatives, designs programs for incumbent worker training, modernization, and future workforce needs in collaboration with workforce development agencies, technical colleges, and community partners. More than forty employers participate. Participants have increased their average annual earnings by 165 percent to more than $22,000 during their first year on the job. The retention rate after four years is more than 70 percent. They are currently branching out into health care and other sectors of the regional economy.

There are hundreds of unionized facilities with labor-management programs that provide worker training. These programs should be encouraged. But most low-wage workers have no union. Other intermediaries should be supported.

Project Quest acts as a go-between for local community colleges and neighborhood residents to create trained workers for employers who in return must provide quality jobs with advancement opportunities.[57] Participants receive tuition and other supports, such as child care, transportation, books and supplies, medical coverage, and counseling. A 1996 evaluation of the program estimated the annual earnings gain of the participants was between $4,900 and $7,500 a year with the expected payoff of costs being a very short three years.[58]

Cooperative Home Care Associates (CHCA), a for-profit, worker-owned cooperative located in the south Bronx, New York, is an example of a program that has attempted to restructure poor-quality jobs in the home health-care industry. The cooperative provides home health-care aides on a contract basis to large health-care providers and major hospitals. The industry learned that investing in frontline workers could provide both better jobs and better patient care. CHCA currently pays workers between $7.00 and $8.00 an hour with health insurance and paid vacation time. Seventy percent of CHCA's employees are employed full-time, and turnover is just 20 percent annually, compared to the industry average of over 60 percent. CHCA provides four weeks of on-site classroom training, plus ninety days of on-the-job training. It also provides home health-care aides a guaranteed minimum number of hours. Most importantly, it provides an ability to become a licensed practical nurse through additional training.[59]

These programs need additional resources. If we are serious about providing lifelong learning, we must find ways to pool private and public resources from which employees can draw funds on an income-based sliding scale. Those monies should be linked to successful programs with proven track records. This more holistic approach to training will ensure that training actually leads to economic improvements.

WORKERS SHOULD BE ASSURED ACCESS TO AFFORDABLE AND SAFE HOUSING

According to a study by the National Low Income Housing Coalition, in some states it would take three times the minimum wage for an individual to rent a two-bedroom apartment at the "fair market rent." [60] At least seven million renters face "critical housing needs" either because they are paying at least 50 percent of their income for rent or are living in too small or substandard units.[61] Most poor-renter households are forced to spend at least half of their income on housing.[62] Still others are out on the street. One-quarter of the 2 to 3.5 million homeless in the United States are working Americans.[63]

It must be ensured that those who qualify for program assistance receive it. Fifteen million American families qualify for federal housing assistance. Only 4.5 million receive that assistance. The Section 8 housing program must be fully funded and provide housing assistance to low-income Americans. At the same time, the supply of affordable housing must be increased.

The United States provides $61 billion in housing subsidies to middle- and higher-income families in the form of mortgage deductions.[64] The yearly total of mortgage deductions is more than four times the Section 8 rental assistance budget, twice that of HUD spending programs, and 19 times as much as the low-income housing tax credits provided to developers of affordable housing.[65] A society that so heavily subsidizes housing for those in the middle and upper reaches of the economy has no business scrimping on help needed for hardworking families at the bottom.

WORKERS SHOULD BE ASSURED A SAFE AND HEALTHY WORKING ENVIRONMENT

Federal law guarantees the right of all workers to a safe and healthy workplace. But low-wage workers face unsafe and unhealthy conditions every day. OSHA must send a strong message, backed up with aggressive enforcement, that unsafe and unhealthy conditions will not be tolerated.

OSHA must also focus its efforts on the most vulnerable workers whom it has largely overlooked in the past, a majority of whom work in smaller workplaces. Worker education and training are an integral part of any efforts. And these efforts must recognize language and other educational barriers. Whistleblower protections must be strengthened. Today, workers who cooperate with OSHA or speak out against hazardous working conditions face years of blacklisting and unemployment while the burdensome legal proceedings take years to complete. That must change.

OSHA must also move forward with a strong ergonomics standard to confront work-related musculoskeletal disorders (MSDs), including repetitive motion injuries, carpal tunnel syndrome, tendonitis, back injuries, and others. MSDs are the single largest category of occupational injuries and illnesses in America today. One million workers lose work time each year from these injuries, which account for more than one in three of the total lost work time cases.[66] A conservative estimate of the cost imposed by MSDs on the American economy (according to the National Academy of Sciences) is between $45 and $54 billion every year. These injuries are also the most severe. According to the Bureau of Labor Statistics, among major disabling injuries and illnesses, median days away from work are the highest for carpal tunnel syndrome (twenty-seven days). Food processing and packing workers, nursing aides, orderlies and attendants, hotel workers, call-center workers, and other low-wage categories suffer more of these disabling injuries than workers in other industries.[67]

Most of these injuries are avoidable. With effective programs and controls, ergonomic injuries can be drastically reduced, according to the 2001 National Research Council and Institute of Medicine Report and the National Academy of Sciences.[68] After implementing an ergonomics program in 1992, for example, Xerox experienced a 24 percent reduction in the number of MSD cases and a 56 percent reduction in direct costs associated with these injuries. 3M reported that following the implementation of an ergonomics program, lost-time injuries from MSDs declined by 58 percent.

Changing the design of tools and workstations, rotating jobs, and other ergonomic interventions such as lift tables and vibration-dampening seating devices reduce the risk of MSDs of the lower back and upper extremities.[69] Employer commitment, employee involvement, identification of problem jobs, analysis and implementation of controls for problem jobs, training and education, and proper medical management are necessary for any program to be effective.[70] But without a governmental standard and enforcement, most companies will do little to change their workplaces to avoid these injuries.

Elizabeth Dole, Labor Secretary under President George H. W. Bush, recognized the need for a standard to confront these hundreds of thousands of disabling injuries and illnesses each year when she initiated rule-making in 1990. It was affirmed by her successor, Lynn Martin. After more than ten years of hearings and debate, an ergonomic standard was finally adopted in January 2001. But congressional Republicans repealed the standard and prohibited enactment of it in its present form. Since 1990, when the ergonomics standard was first promised, more than six million workers have suffered serious injuries from exposure to ergonomic hazards on the job.[71]

OSHA must once again move forward with a new standard. In the meantime, it must vigorously confront ergonomic problems in these workplaces under OSHA's general duty clause that "requires employers to provide workplaces free from recognized hazards that cause or are likely to cause death or serious physical harm."

WORKERS MUST BE ASSURED SECURITY IN TIME OF ECONOMIC ADVERSITY AND RETIREMENT

ALL WORKERS NEED FINANCIAL SUPPORT DURING TIMES OF UNEMPLOYMENT

Job insecurity, a problem for all Americans in today's economy, is particularly pervasive in low-wage jobs. Workers in these jobs suffer the most frequent periods of unemployment and must face these periods with little or no employer-provided severance pay or other benefits to cushion the blow. At the same time, they are half as likely as higher-wage workers to qualify for unemployment insurance.[72] Unemployment laws discriminate against the very workers who need them the most: lower-income working Americans.

To respond to this problem, employers should be required to provide workers severance pay equal to two weeks of pay upon the loss of a job.[73] With little savings, severance pay is essential to these workers and their families' well-being. Unemployment compensation laws must be revised to eliminate the discrimination against lower-wage workers and workers who work less than full-time hours. It must also be redesigned to reflect a more mobile workforce and the reality that most people who are out of work will not return to their former employer.

Generally, state laws provide that unemployed workers must fulfill three general conditions to qualify for benefits. Workers must have been "substantially attached" to the labor market; they must have left their prior job involuntarily or have quit their job for "good cause" only; and they must be currently "able and available" for work and—in most states—actively seeking work.[74]

States have conservatively interpreted these requirements to limit the eligibility for low-wage workers. States require minimum amounts of earnings and hours to satisfy being fully attached to the employer. Yet low-wage employers provide their workers the fewest hours. To qualify, workers must show "good cause" for leaving their job, which has been narrowly interpreted so that only work-related circumstances make workers eligible. But in many low-wage situations, workers leave their jobs because of inadequate child care, lack of transportation, or domestic violence—circumstances that would not qualify an individual for unemployment insurance benefits in most states. And most states require an individual to be looking for full-time work to actually qualify. This requirement disqualifies many women who cannot work full-time because of family responsibilities.[75]

To eliminate the discrimination against lower-wage workers, the earnings requirement for unemployment benefits should be eliminated or reframed in terms of number of hours. The requirement of "good cause" must be extended to include domestic violence, family illness, and the lack of child care and transportation. Workers should not be disqualified if they are seeking part-time work. And benefits should be increased.

Because most workers today do not return to their prior employer, the system must be revamped to adjust to this new reality. Individuals out of work today in most cases need retraining, a longer time to find another job, and health coverage during that period. The Trade Adjustment Act is a good model providing workers extended unemployment, health coverage, and training assistance.

AMERICANS SHOULD BE SECURE IN THEIR RETIREMENT

The United States retirement system has been likened to a three-legged stool.[76] Social Security provides one leg, private pensions the second, and private savings the third. Each leg is needed to ensure a secure retirement. Since 1970 the percentage of private sector workforce participation in pension plans has hovered at around 50 percent. Yet the participation rate is heavily skewed based on income. For workers with incomes of less than $20,000 a year, only 20 percent participate in a pension plan. In contrast, 80 percent of workers with incomes above $50,000 are offered a plan, and 90 percent participate. The top 40 percent of wage earners receive more than 70 percent of the total pension benefits and hold more than 70 percent of the pension wealth. For those in the bottom 20 percent, pensions account for only 3 percent of their retirement income at age sixty-five and over.[77] And low-wage workers have little or no savings. They enter retirement wobbling on one leg.

If Social Security provided sufficient income for lower-income workers to meet their basic retirement needs, the lack of pension coverage and savings would not be an issue. But Social Security is inadequate. On average, it replaces only 55 percent of a couple's income for those in the bottom 20 percent of wage earners, forcing them to continue working. Low-wage jobs are hard, even on young people. At retirement age, it is devastating that these workers must continue to stoop, cut, lift, and do the difficult work required by most of these jobs.

Americans in pension plans receive $70 to $80 billion in government subsidies. Their employer pension contributions and the buildup in their pension plans are not taxed. Most of these subsidies go to families earning more than $100,000 a year. It is only fair that the retirement for lower-end workers—who are not the beneficiaries of these subsidies—should be supplemented.

In developing a strategy for improving retirement income for low-wage workers, a variety of considerations should be taken into account.[78] Most lower-end workers are in firms that do not offer pension plans. Even if they are offered pension plans, they will need assistance in contributing.

A retirement mechanism that is not attached to a single employer makes the most sense, since most employers of low-wage workers do not offer a pension plan and these workers are the most mobile. One example might be something similar to President Clinton's proposed "Universal Savings Accounts" (USA), in which families earning less than $40,000 would get an annual $600 tax credit deposited directly into their USA account, plus another $700 if they deposited $700 of their own money into the account. It could be set up in the style of TIAA-CREF so that the accounts would have the advantage of being a part of a large investment fund.

Another approach for workers whose employers offer a 401(k) plan is a reverse match in which an employer's 401(k) plan would only qualify for tax status if it enrolled all its workers and provided minimum contributions (perhaps 1–3 percent to all employees).[79] Employees then would have the option of matching their employers' contributions. There are a variety of approaches. What is important is that lower-end workers have enough retirement income at the end of their work lives to sustain themselves and their families.

WORKERS MUST BE ASSURED THE RIGHT TO ORGANIZE AND COLLECTIVELY BARGAIN

Labor unions provide the most direct means to correct the daily imbalance of power between workers and their employers and to improve the quality of low-wage jobs. Yet significant barriers constrain workers' attempts to organize. The unfettered right to organize and bargain collectively must be assured. Correcting this situation would not be difficult. It simply takes a desire to eliminate these barriers.

The organizing and bargaining process should be simplified and expedited. Workers who want to be represented by a union would sign a card or petition authorizing representation. If a majority of the workers signed such a card, the National Labor Relations Board (NLRB), or some other impartial observer would certify the results, and the workers would be unionized. Bargaining units should reflect the changes in the workplace and be broadly defined to include contingent and nonstandard workers. Any procedure should have safeguards to ensure that signing a card genuinely reflects a worker's free choice.

Workers should have the right to receive information from union representatives at their workplaces. Immigrants should not have to face any questions regarding their immigration status during an organizing campaign. Immigration laws should not be used to destroy a worker's fundamental right of freedom of association, nor should it be used to shield an employer in violation of labor laws.

In contrast to the minor penalties that employers currently face when they harass, intimidate, or fire workers for union activities, any employer threats or intimidation should receive strong and swift remedies. When the NLRB's investigation finds merit in a worker's charge of discriminatory discharge, the worker should be immediately reinstated while litigation continues. Only such an interim measure can overcome the devastating impact on the worker who is dismissed and eliminate the chilling effect on the overall organizing effort. Abuses should also carry meaningful penalties so that remedies and sanctions act as deterrents. Workers should receive full back pay regardless of their interim earnings. Employers should pay substantial fines and punitive damages and be prohibited from receiving public monies in cases of willful legal violations.[80] Bargaining should begin immediately upon certification, regardless of employer challenges.[81] There must be a mechanism—such as first contract arbitration—to ensure that workers are not frustrated by an employer who stalls to prevent a contract.

The labor movement must also do its part by strategically committing resources to organizing, developing a political strategy to enhance that organizing, becoming real members and allies in their communities, and creatively responding to the needs of these workers.

WORKERS SHOULD BE ASSURED FAIR TRADE AND IMMIGRATION POLICIES

TRADE

There is a race to the bottom in how workers are treated in the name of global competition. In order to stop such a race, standards must be enforced that reflect our core values. Should American workers be forced to compete with child labor or prison labor? Should American workers be forced to compete with countries who prohibit their workers from organizing and collectively bargaining? We must ensure that basic human values are applied to international trade.

The International Labour Organization, a tripartite labor-business-government agency whose participating countries include the United States, has already approved a group of "core worker rights."[82] They include: freedom of association; the effective recognition of the right to collective bargaining; the elimination of all forms of forced or compulsory labor; the effective abolition of child labor; and the elimination of discrimination in respect to employment and occupation.[83] Each ILO country is committed to "respect, to promote and to realize in good faith and in accordance with the Constitution, the principles concerning the fundamental rights which are the subject of those Conventions."[84]

ILO Director-General Juan Somavia recognized the importance of these core rights in "hasten[ing] the elimination of the most inhumane labor practices" in today's global economy.[85] Guaranteeing core labor standards would "create the negotiating power necessary to eliminate the many forms of unacceptable labor practices that still exist whether in export industries or elsewhere in the economy." This "countervailing power," he said, can also help redress "the central problem of an uneven distribution of the gains from trade and economic growth." [86]

These "core labor rights" should form a minimum basis for global trade and should be included in any trade agreement in which the United States takes part. Worker rights provisions that already exist in current trade laws should be vigorously enforced.[87] Other institutions, such as the International Monetary Fund and the World Bank, could condition loans on the adherence to these "core labor rights," and thus strengthen the incentive for countries to adhere to these standards.

These suggestions are not meant to be comprehensive. They are an attempt to identify some minimum standards that should form the basis of our global trade. Trade agreements should be structured to ensure that the playing field is fair to American workers. Without standards, global competition will merely be a race to the bottom that encourages the worst forms of human practices. These will hurt not only workers in less-developed countries who are forced to work under those circumstances, but also American workers forced to compete at that level.

IMMIGRATION

Immigrants are critical to the United States economy, accounting for one out of every two new workers in the past decade.[88] Many of those immigrants are in the United States without legal papers. While the U.S. benefits from their labor, these immigrants must work with the lingering threat of deportation, leaving them with little bargaining power. The result is a system with submarket wages and harsh working conditions for undocumented workers and for those who compete with them in the labor market.[89]

Continuing the current harsh policy on illegal immigration fails to serve American interests. An underground economy has been created, with all of its exploitive characteristics. It is a policy that is unfair to those who work in our economy and ill serves our national security by keeping a large part of our population in the shadows. There must be movement from a black market to a transparent, regulated system. A reformed system would grant legal status to workers already here through some kind of earned legalization program, create a legal channel for future workers to enter the U.S. with appropriate worker safeguards, and stiffly penalize those who continue to illegally profit from the exploitation of immigrants.[90]

CONCLUSION

This compact with working Americans rewards work and responds to the daily deprivations of millions of working Americans and their families. Whether we will be a nation of opportunity and justice for all or one in which only the few prosper at the expense of millions of workers and their families is ultimately up to us. Many argue that these improvements will cost too much. But the cost of doing nothing is even greater. It denies workers the essentials of a decent life and subjects their children to such deprivations that they have little chance of success. It hurts our economy, it hurts our democracy, and it hurts our health as a nation if we ignore those who are working hard but getting shortchanged. It prevents these American workers from becoming real stakeholders in their communities. And to tolerate this injustice demeans us as people.

Certainly we must always evaluate cost. But widely different standards of cost depending on the recipients of the benefits are tolerated. There is little thought given to the costs of the subsidies we give to the middle class and the wealthy. When was the last time there was a mainstream debate about the $61 billion in tax deductions for home mortgages or the $140 billion in health insurance tax exemptions and deductions or the $70–80 billion in pension deductions?[91]

There is little public controversy about the billions of dollars the United States provides in corporate welfare—estimated at $125 billion a year by the federal government alone—in the form of tax abatements, price supports, tax shelters, and subsidies.[92] Corporations receive subsidies for everything from selling weapons overseas to crop insurance for tobacco. Cost is largely disregarded when it comes to the wealthy and corporations. Yet when it comes to hardworking, less fortunate Americans, cost gets center stage.

Today, work fails millions of American workers and their families. However we distribute the responsibilities between workers, employers, and government, we can no longer pretend that if the problem is ignored it will disappear. There is no option—whether by default or collective action, we decide what happens to these millions of invisible Americans. We can fulfill the promise that if you are willing to work hard, you can provide the basic necessities for you and your family. As Michael Harrington wrote, "The means are at hand." The question is whether we have the will.

NOTES

CHAPTER 2: PILING ON: WHY IT'S ABOUT MORE THAN MONEY

1. Henry S. Farber and Helen Levy, *Recent Trends in Employer Sponsored Health Insurance Coverage: Are Bad Jobs Getting Worse?*, Working Paper 6709, National Bureau of Economic Research, August 1998; Pierce Brooks, *Compensation Inequality*, unpublished manuscript, Bureau of Labor Statistics, April 1998; Daniel S. Hamermesh, *Changing Inequality in Markets for Workplace Amenities*, Working Paper 6515, National Bureau of Economic Research, April 1998; Peter Passell, "Benefits Dwindle Along With Wages for the Unskilled," *The New York Times*, June 14, 1998.

2. See Lawrence Mishel, Jared Bernstein, and John Schmitt, *The State of Working America 2002–2003* (Ithaca, NY: Cornell University Press, 2002); Anthony P. Carnevale and Stephen J. Rose, "Low-Earners: Who are They? Do They Have a Way Out?" in Richard Kazis and Marc S. Miller, eds., *Low-Wage Workers in the New Economy* (Washington, DC: Urban Institute Press, 2001), found that forty-six million workers make less than $15,000 a year.

3. Mishel, et al., *The State of Working America 2002–2003*.

4. Neil Irwin and Nicholas Johnston, "A Job Market Divided by

Skill: Low-Tech Workers Vulnerable as Some Local Employers Cut Positions," *The Washington Post,* September 24, 2001; Jonathan Eig, "Do Part-Time Workers Hold Key to When the Recession Breaks," *The Wall Street Journal,* January 3, 2002.

5. Richard B. Freeman, *When Earnings Diverge: Causes, Consequences, and Cures for the New Inequality in the U.S.,* Commissioned by the Committee on New Realities of the National Policy Association, NPA Report #284 (1997); Timothy M. Smeeding, "U.S. Income Inequality in a Cross-National Perspective: Why Are We So Different?," in *The Inequality Paradox: Growth of Income Disparity,* National Policy Association Report #288, 1998; Michael C. Wolfson and Brian B. Murphy, "New View on Inequality Trends in Canada and the United States," *Monthly Labor Review,* April 1998.

6. Lawrence Mishel, Jared Bernstein, and John Schmitt, *The State of Working America 2000–2001* (Ithaca, NY: Cornell University Press, 2001).

7. Ibid.

8. Smeeding, "U.S. Income Inequality in a Cross-National Perspective."

9. Heather Boushey, Chauna Brocht, Bethney Gundersen, and Jared Bernstein, *Hardships in America: The Real Story of Working Families,* Economic Policy Institute, 2001.

10. John E. Schwartz, *Illusions of Opportunity: The American Dream in Question* (New York: W.W. Norton & Company, 1997). See also the Family Economic Self-Sufficiency Project, a project of Wider Opportunities for Women, which provides resources and technical assistance in support of community-based strategies for creating self-sufficiency for low-income families, at http://www.sixstrategies.org. Edmund S. Phelps, *Rewarding Work: How to Restore Participation and Self Support to Free Enterprise* (Cambridge, MA: Harvard University Press, 1997).

11. Constance F. Citro and Robert T. Michael, *Measuring Poverty:*

A New Approach (Washington, DC: National Academy Press, 1995); Boushey, et al., *Hardships in America*.

12. Joel F. Handler, "Low-Wage Work As We Know It: What's Wrong/What Can Be Done," in Joel F. Handler and Lucie White, eds. *Hard Labor* (Armonk, NY: M.E. Sharpe, 1999).

13. Boushey, et al., *Hardships in America*. Isabel Sawhill, a Brookings Institution economist and expert in the area of poverty and the low-wage labor market, concludes that those who live below 100 percent of the poverty line, what she terms the "poor," and those who live between 100–200 percent of poverty, the "near poor," are both in need of support. Isabel Sawhill and Adam Thomas, *A Hand Up for the Bottom Third: Toward a New Agenda for Low-Income Working Families* (Washington, DC: Brookings Institution, 2000). Gregory Acs and Katherin Ross Phillips of the Urban Institute conclude that 200 percent of poverty is a more accurate standard for whether a family of four is low-income. Gregory Acs, Katherin Ross Phillips, and Daniel McKenzie, "Playing by the Rules, but Losing the Game: Americans in Low-Income Working Families," in *Low-Wage Workers in the New Economy*.

14. Using different data and different definitions of who is working, Carnevale and Rose, in "Low-Earners," found a similar number of low-wage workers in low-income families. They found that twenty million low-wage workers were in families that had incomes of $25,000 or less.

15. Maya Federman, Thesia I. Garner, Kathleen Short, W. Boman Cutter IV, John Kiely, David Levine, Duane McGough, and Marilyn McMillen, "What Does it Mean to be Poor in America?" *Monthly Labor Review*, May 1996.

16. Boushey, et al., *Hardships in America*.

17. *Out of Reach: America's Growing Wage-Rent Disparity*, National Low Income Housing Coalition/LIHIS, September 2001; *Housing Costs Out of Reach for Many: 2002 National Housing Wage is*

$14.66, National Low Income Housing Coalition/LIHIS, September 18, 2002.

18. Federman, et al., "What Does it Mean to be Poor in America?"

19. Ibid.

20. Ibid.

21. Boushey, et al., *Hardships in America.*

22. Gregory Acs and Eugene Steuerle, "The Corporation as a Dispenser of Welfare and Security," in Carl Kaysen, ed., *The American Corporation Today* (New York: Oxford University Press, 1996).

23. Jack Meyer and Diane Naughton, *Assessing Business Attitudes on Health Care*, Economic and Social Research Institute, October 1996.

24. Paul Fronstin, *Sources of Health Insurance and Characteristics of the Uninsured: Analysis of the March 1996 Current Population Survey*, Issue Brief No. 179, Employee Benefit Research Institute, Washington, DC, 1996; *Poverty Rates Fall, But Remain High for a Period with Such Low Unemployment*, Center on Budget and Policy Priorities Report, October 8, 1998.

25. *Employee Benefits Research Institute Databook on Employee Benefits*, 1997; Barbara Schone and Philip Cooper, Kaiser Commission, Agency for Health Care Policy and Research, part of the Department of Health and Human Services Study, *Health Affairs*, November 10, 1997.

26. Paul B. Ginsburg, Jon R. Gabel, and Kelly A. Hunt, "Tracing Small-Firm Coverage, 1989–1996," *Health Affairs*, January/February 1998; Fronstin, *Sources of Health Insurance and Characteristics of the Uninsured: Analysis of the March 1997 Current Population Survey*, Employee Benefit Research Institute, Washington, DC, December 1997; Kaiser Family Foundation, *Changes in Employee Health Coverage by Small Businesses*, February 1999.

27. *EBRI Data Book on Employee Benefits*, 1997.

28. Elliot K. Wicks and Jack A. Meyer, *Covering America: Real Remedies for the Uninsured*, Economic and Social Research Institute Occasional Paper, December 2001.

29. *Employee Medical Care Contributions on the Rise*, U.S. Department of Labor, Bureau of Labor Statistics, April 1998. The average annual contributions for larger firms is less, $408 per year for single coverage and close to $1,500 for family coverage; Ginsburg, et al., "Tracing Small-Firm Coverage, 1989–1996."

30. Jack Meyer and Sharon Silow-Carroll, *Policy Options to Assure Access to Health Care for People Leaving Welfare for Work*, Economic and Social Research Institute Report, September 1996.

31. Ibid.

32. Farber and Levy, *Recent Trends in Employer-Sponsored Health Insurance Coverage*; Meyer and Naughton, *Assessing Business Attitudes on Health Care*.

33. William J. Wiatrowski, "Who Really has Access to Employer-Provided Health Benefits?," *Monthly Labor Review*, June 1995.

34. John Z. Ayanian, Joel S. Weissman, Eric C. Schneider, Jack A. Ginsburg, and Alan M. Zaslavsky, "Unmet Health Needs of Uninsured Adults in the United States," *Journal of the American Medical Association*, Vol. 284, No. 16, October 25, 2000.

35. *Employee Benefits in Small Private Industry Establishment*, 1996, Bureau of Labor Statistics; *BLS Reports on Employee Benefits in Medium and Large Private Establishments*, 1995.

36. Dora L. Costa, *The Unequal Work Day: A Long-Term View*, Working Paper 6419, National Bureau of Economic Research, February 1998.

37. *Contingent Workers: Incomes and Benefits Lag Behind Those of Rest of Workforce*, GAO Report, June 2000, GAO/HEHS-00-76; Lawrence Mishel, Jared Bernstein, and John Schmitt, *The State of Working America, 1998–1999* (Ithaca, NY: Cornell University Press, 1999).

38. Mishel, et al., *The State of Working America 2000–2001*; Roberta Spalter-Roth and Heidi Hartmann, "Gauging the Consequences for Gender Relations, Pay Equity, and the Public Purse," in Kathleen Barker and Kathleen Christensen, eds., *Contingent Work:*

American Employment Relations in Transition (Ithaca, NY: Cornell University Press, 1998); Juliet B. Schor, *The Overworked American* (New York, Basic Books, 1992).

39. *Contingent Workers: Incomes and Benefits Lag Behind Those of Rest of Workforce*, GAO Report.

40. Joan Williams, *Unbending Gender: Why Family and Work Conflict and What to Do About It* (Oxford: Oxford University Press, 2000).

41. *Contingent Workers*; Williams, *Unbending Gender*.

42. Mishel, et al., *The State of Working America 2000–2001*.

43. *Contingent Workers*.

44. Spalter-Roth and Hartmann, "Gauging the Consequences for Gender Relations, Pay Equity, and the Public Purse."

45. Richard S. Belous, "The Rise of the Contingent Workforce: Growth of Temporary, Part-Time, and Subcontracted Employment," *Looking Ahead*, Vol. XIX, No. 1, June 1997, National Policy Association.

46. Ibid.

47. Ibid.; and *Contingent Workers*.

48. *Contingent Workers*.

49. "Working at Odd Hours," *Federal Reserve Bank of Boston Regional Review*, Vol. 8, No. 1, Q1, 1998; Daniel S. Hamermesh, "The Timing of Work Over Time," *The Economic Journal*, January 1999, Vol. 109, 37–66; Hamermesh, *Changing Inequality in Markets for Workplace Amenities*, NBER Working Paper Series, Working Paper 6515, NBER, April 1998.

50. "Working at Odd Hours"; Hamermesh, "The Timing of Work Over Time."

51. Hamermesh, "The Timing of Work Over Time."

52. Jody Heymann, *The Widening Gap: Why America's Working Families Are in Jeopardy and What Can Be Done About It* (New York: Basic Books, 2000).

53. Ellen Galinsky and James T. Bond, "Helping Families with Young Children Navigate Work and Family Life," Families and Work

Institute, based on "Supporting Families as Primary Caregivers: The Role of the Workplace" in D. Cryer and H. Harms, eds., *Research into Practice in Infant/Toddler Care* (Baltimore: Brookes Publishing Co., forthcoming).

54. *Employee Benefits in Small Private Industry Establishments, 1996,* Bureau of Labor Statistics. *Reports on Employee Benefits in Medium and Large Private Establishments,* Bureau of Labor Statistics, 1995.

55. Ibid.

56. Peter Passell, "Benefits Dwindle Along with Wages," *The New York Times,* June 14, 1998.

57. Galinsky and Bond, "Helping Families with Young Children Navigate Work and Family Life."

58. Ibid.

59. *Contingent Workers.*

60. Lynn Olson, "Starting Early," in "Quality Counts 2002: Building Blocks for Success," *Education Week,* Vol. 21, No. 16, January 10, 2002; Isabel V. Sawhill, *Investing in Children,* Children's Roundtable Report #1, Brookings Institution, April 1999; Galinsky and Bond, "Helping Families with Young Children Navigate Work and Family Life." Paying for adult supervision for public school-age children, while less costly than child care, is still difficult for these workers to afford. Few schools provide on-site care.

61. Employer-provided benefits such as child-care resource and referral services, on- or near-site child care, and direct financial child-care assistance are still rare. If they are provided, however, they are provided to higher-paid workers. These high-end workers also get the benefit of employer-provided dependent care assistance plans. Under these plans, employees may set aside part of their pretax wages in an account that can be used to pay for child care. Galinsky and Bond, "Helping Families with Young Children Navigate Work and Family Life."

62. Vicky Lowell and Heidi Hartmann, "Increasing Economic Se-

curity for Low-Wage Women Workers," in Kazis and Miller, eds., *Low-Wage Workers in the New Economy*.

63. Sara S. McLanahan, Nan Marie Astone, and Nadine F. Marks, "The Role of Mother-Only Families in Reproducing Poverty," in Aletha C. Huston, ed., *Children in Poverty: Child Development and Public Policy* (Cambridge: Cambridge University Press, 1991), 51–78; Deborah A. Phillips, "With a Little Help: Children in Poverty and Child Care," in Huston, ed., *Children in Poverty*, 159–191; Arloc Sherman, *Wasting America's Future* (Boston: Beacon Press, 1994).

64. Galinsky and Bond, "Helping Families with Young Children Navigate Work and Family Life."

65. Harriet Presser, "Toward a 24 Hour Economy," *Science* 284 (1999), 1778.

66. Mishel, et al., *The State of Working America 2000–2001*.

67. "Working at Odd Hours"; Sawhill, *Investing In Children*. Child-care centers that are open at night or early morning are rare and costly, and in-home care is hard to find during these hours.

68. Hamermesh, *Changing Inequality in Markets for Workplace Amenities*.

69. *Food Processing, Packing and Manufacturing Update*, UFCW Special Report, March 1998.

70. Ibid.

71. Ibid.; *The Disposable Workforce: A Worker's Perspective*, A Documentation Study Conducted by the Public Justice Center of Working Conditions in Delmarva Poultry Processing Plants, Public Justice Center, 1998.

72. Sarah O. Campany and Martin E. Personick, "Profiles in Safety and Health: Retail Grocery Stores," *Monthly Labor Review*, Washington, DC, September 1992.

73. Bureau of Labor Statistics, *Issues*, August 1994.

74. Abdella Mutawe, Ronald Tsunehara, Jerrold Hackett, and Mark Hatch, "Occupational Health & Safety Compliance in Nursing Homes," *Professional Safety*, November 2000, Vol. 45, No. 11, 18–21.

75. Michele Picard, "Working Under an Electronic Thumb," *Training,* February 1994.

76. Sarah Schafer, "Home Life on Hold?: Verizon Strikers Say Call Centers Take Toll," *The Washington Post,* August 18, 2000.

77. *The Disposable Workforce.*

78. *EBRI Databook on Employee Benefits,* 4th Edition, 1997.

79. Laurie J. Bassie, Anne L. Gallagher, and Ed Schroer, *The ASTD Training DataBook* (Alexandria, VA: American Society for Training and Development, 1996).

80. Ibid.

81. Phelps, *Rewarding Work.*

82. Neil Irwin and Nicholas Johnston, "A Job Market Divided by Skill: Low-Tech Workers Vulnerable as Some Local Employers Cut Positions," *The Washington Post,* September 24, 2001.

83. Peter Cappelli, Laurie Bassi, Harry Katz, David Knoke, Paul Osterman, and Michael Useem, *Change at Work* (New York: Oxford University Press, 1997).

84. Sharon Dietrich, Maurice Emsellem, and Catherine Ruckelshaus, "Work Reform: The Other Side of Welfare Reform," *Stanford Law and Policy Review,* Vol. 9, No. 1 1998. Many low-wage workers lack information about their eligibility for unemployment compensation. Their employers are not required to furnish them information. And if they receive benefits, the amount of money received is a fraction of one's prior income. A number of reasons contributed to a decline in unemployment compensation, including a decline in the manufacturing sector, decline in unionization resulting in less information to workers concerning unemployment compensation, federal and state policy changes, which made eligibility requirements more stringent, and broad demographic changes. Daniel P. McMurrer and Amy B. Chasanov, "Trends in Unemployment Insurance Benefits," *Monthly Labor Review,* September 1995.

85. McMurrer and Chasanov, "Trends in Unemployment Insurance Benefits."

86. *EBRI Databook on Employee Benefits.*

87. Ibid.

88. Ibid.

89. *Pension Plans: Characteristics of Persons in the Labor Force Without Pension Coverage,* GAO Report, August 2000, GAO/HEHS-00-131.

CHAPTER 3: IN THE HEART OF OUR ECONOMY AND OUR LIVES

1. The 5 percent figure includes 500,000 fast-food cooks and all 1.5 million food preparation and services workers. The food preparation and service workers are not limited to fast-food restaurants. Accordingly, the 5 percent figure is an overestimate of the actual number.

2. Cameron Lynne Macdonald and Carmen Sirianni, "The Service Society and the Changing Experience of Work," in Cameron Lynne Macdonald and Carmen Sirianni, eds., *Working in the Service Society* (Philadelphia: Temple University Press, 1996).

3. Paul Ryscavage, *Income Inequality in America: An Analysis of Trends* (Armonk, NY: M.E. Sharpe, 1999).

4. Bureau of Labor Statistics, *BLS Releases New 1998–2008 Employment Projections,* November 30, 1999.

5. Richard B. Freeman, *When Earnings Diverge: Causes, Consequences, and Cures for the New Inequality in the U.S.,* NPA Report #284 (Washington, DC: National Policy Association, 1997); Gail Foster and Lynn Franco, "Perspectives on Income Disparity," in James Auerbach and Richard Belous, *The Inequality Paradox: Growth of Income Disparity* (Washington, DC: National Policy Association, 1998); Lawrence Mishel, Jared Bernstein, and John Schmitt, *The State of Working America 1998–1999* (Ithaca, NY: Cornell University Press, 1999).

6. Richard W. Judy and Carol D. Amici, *Workforce 2020: Work and Workers in the 21st Century* (Indianapolis: Hudson Institute, 1997).

7. Frank Levy, *The New Dollars and Dreams: American Incomes and Economic Change* (New York: The Russell Sage Foundation, 1998).

8. Peter Cappelli, et al., *Change at Work* (New York: Oxford University Press, 1997).

9. Levy, *The New Dollars and Dreams.* Transportation, communications, and utilities account for 6.6 million jobs; wholesale trade accounts for 6.8 million jobs; retail trade accounts for 22.7 million jobs; finance, insurance, and real estate accounts for 7.4 million jobs; federal, state, and local government accounts for 20 million jobs; and services accounts for 38 million jobs. *Economic Report of the President, Transmitted to the Congress, February 1999, Together with the Annual Report of the Council of Economic Advisors* (Washington, DC: U.S. Government Printing Office, 1999).

10. Levy, *The New Dollars and Dreams*; Ryscavage, *Income Inequality in America.* Executive, administrative, and managerial occupations will add 2.4 million jobs, and professional specialty occupations are expected to add 5.3 million. Douglas Braddock, "Employment Outlook: 1998–2008, Occupational Employment Projections to 2008," *Monthly Labor Review,* November 1999.

11. Stephen A. Herzenberg, John A. Alic, and Howard Wial, *New Rules for a New Economy: Employment and Opportunity in Postindustrial America* (Ithaca, NY: Cornell University Press, 1998); *1996 National Occupational Employment and Wage Data,* Bureau of Labor Statistics, U.S. Department of Labor, 1996.

12. Thirty-nine percent of the transportation sector, 26 percent of the telecommunications sector, 34 percent of the utilities sector, 41 percent of the education sector, and 37 percent of the public administration sector are organized, as compared to only a 16 percent unionization rate in the overall economy. Herzenberg, et al., *New Rules for a New Economy.*

13. Allison Thomson, "Employment Outlook 1998–2008: Industry Output and Employment Projections to 2008," *Monthly Labor Re-*

view, November 1999. Retail trade has twenty-two million jobs and the services have thirty-seven million jobs.

14. *Economic Report of the President, Transmitted to the Congress, February 1999, Together with the Annual Report of the Council of Economic Advisers.*

15. Herzenberg, et al., *New Rules for a New Economy.*

16. Personal and entertainment and recreation services have the same high levels as retail trade—34 and 37 percent respectively. These figures compare to 5 percent of part-time jobs in manufacturing. Herzenberg, et al., *New Rules for a New Economy.*

17. I have used the average number of part-time hours according to the Bureau of Labor Statistics, which is 20.6, to determine what the part-time salary would be.

18. Jared Bernstein and Heidi Hartmann, "Defining and Characterizing the Low-Wage Labor Market," in *The Low-Wage Labor Market: Challenges and Opportunities for Economic Self-Sufficiency*, U.S. Department of Health and Human Services, Office of the Secretary, Assistant Secretary for Planning and Evaluation, Washington, DC, December 1999; Herzenberg, et al., *New Rules for a New Economy.*

19. Jay M. Berman, "Employment Outlook: 2000–2010: Industry Output and Employment Projections to 2010," *Monthly Labor Review*, November 2001.

20. Daniel E. Hecker, "Occupational Employment Projections to 2010," *Monthly Labor Review*, November 2001.

21. Berman, "Employment Outlook: 2000–2010: Industry Output and Employment Projections to 2010."

22. Hecker, "Occupational Employment Projections to 2010."

23. Ibid.

24. Ibid.

25. Communication Workers of America, AFL-CIO, Research Department, *Customer Service Professionals: A Key Occupation in the Information Age*, August 1997.

26. *1997 National Occupational Employment and Wage Estimates,*

Bureau of Labor Statistics, U.S. Department of Labor. This data set uses $8.50 as a cutoff rather than $8.70. Obviously, if the $8.70 figures were used, there would be slightly higher numbers.

27. *1997 National Occupational Employment and Wage Estimates.*

28. Hecker, "Occupational Employment Projections to 2010."

29. T.R. Swartz and K.M. Weigert, eds., *America's Working Poor: 1980–1990* (Notre Dame, IN: University of Notre Dame Press, 1995).

30. Center for the Child Care Workforce, *Current Data on Child Care Salaries and Benefits in the United States,* March 1998.

31. Ibid.

32. Hecker, "Occupational Employment Projections to 2010."

33. *1997 National Occupational Employment and Wage Estimates.*

34. United Food and Commercial Workers International Union, *Food Processing, Packing and Manufacturing Update Special Report,* March 1998.

35. Ibid.

36. *1997 National Occupational Employment and Wage Estimates.*

37. Ibid.

38. George T. Silvestri, "Employment Outlook: 1996–2006 Occupational Employment Projections to 2006," *Monthly Labor Review,* November 1997.

39. Hecker, "Occupational Employment Projections to 2010."

40. John J. Kane and Martin E. Personick, "Profiles in Safety and Health: Hotels and Motels," *Monthly Labor Review,* July 1993.

41. *1997 National Occupational Employment and Wage Estimates.*

42. Kane and Personick, "Profiles in Safety and Health."

43. *Employment and Earnings,* Bureau of Labor Statistics, October 1996.

44. Lawrence Mishel, Jared Bernstein, and John Schmitt, *The State of Working America 1996–1997,* Economic Policy Institute (Armonk, NY: M.E. Sharpe, 1997).

45. Silvestri, "Employment Outlook: 1996–2006."

46. *1997 National Occupational Employment and Wage Estimates.*

47. *Employment and Earnings.*

48. Thomas Bailey and Annette Bernhardt, "In Search of the High Road in a Low-Wage Industry," *Politics and Society,* Vol. 25, No. 2, June 1997.

49. *1997 National Occupational Employment and Wage Estimates;* and Silvestri, "Employment Outlook: 1996–2006."

CHAPTER 4: THE DEMOGRAPHY OF A CASTE

1. Gregory Acs, Katherin Ross Phillips, and Daniel McKenzie, "Playing by the Rules, but Losing the Game: Americans in Low-Income Working Families," in Richard Kazis and Marc S. Miller, eds., *Low-Wage Workers in the New Economy* (Washington, DC: The Urban Institute Press, 2001); Lawrence Mishel, Jared Bernstein, and Heather Boushey, *The State of Working America 2002–2003* (Ithaca, NY: Cornell University Press, 2002); Jared Bernstein, "The Low-Wage Labor Market: Trends and Policy Implications," written for the Penn State University 2002 National Symposium on Family Issues: Work Family Challenges for Low-Income Parents and their Children.

2. Mishel, et al., *The State of Working America 2002–2003;* Richard B. Freeman, "Is the New Income Inequality the Achilles' Heel of the American Economy," in James A. Auerbach and Richard Belous, eds., *The Inequality Paradox: Growth of Income Disparity,* National Policy Association Report #288, Washington, DC, 1998; Paul Ryscavage, *Income Inequality in America: An Analysis of Trends* (Armonk, NY: M.E. Sharpe, 1999).

3. Whites are the only group statistically underrepresented in low-wage jobs, making up 73.6 percent of the workforce, yet 63 percent of low-wage workers. Jared Bernstein and Heidi Hartmann, "Defining and Characterizing the Low-Wage Labor Market," in *The Low-Wage Labor Market: Challenges and Opportunities for Economic Self-Sufficiency,* U.S. Department of Health and Human Services, Office of the Secretary, Assistant Secretary for Planning and Evaluation, Washington, DC, December 1999.

4. Bernstein and Hartmann, "Defining and Characterizing the Low-Wage Labor Market."

5. Mishel, et al., *The State of Working America 2002–2003*; Bernstein and Hartmann, "Defining and Characterizing the Low-Wage Labor Market."

6. Women are overrepresented in low-wage jobs. They make up 47 percent of the workforce and 60 percent of the low-wage workforce. Bernstein and Hartmann, "Defining and Characterizing the Low-Wage Labor Market."

7. Mishel, et al., *The State of Working America 2002–2003*.

8. According to the U.S. *Current Population Survey*, median weekly earnings of full-time male workers have dropped by 13 percent from 1979 through the mid-nineties. U.S. men have lost ground compared to other industrial countries. In Western Europe, male workers in the bottom 10 percent of the earnings distribution earn 68 percent of the median workers' income, in Japan, that figure is 61 percent. In the U.S., male workers earn only 38 percent of the median. Richard B. Freeman, *When Earnings Diverge: Causes, Consequences, and Cures for the New Inequality in the U.S.*, National Policy Association Report #284, Washington, DC, 1997; Bernstein and Hartmann, "Defining and Characterizing the Low-Wage Labor Market."

9. Mishel, et al., *The State of Working America 2002–2003*.

10. Lawrence Mishel, Jared Bernstein, and John Schmitt, *The State of Working America 1998–1999* (Ithaca, NY: Cornell University Press, 1999).

11. Acs, et al., "Playing by the Rules, but Losing the Game."

12. Bernstein and Hartmann, "Defining and Characterizing the Low-Wage Labor Market."

13. Jared Bernstein, "Demand Shifts and Low-wage Workers," *Eastern Economic Journal*, Spring 1999; Lawrence Mishel, Jared Bernstein, and John Schmitt, *The State of Working America 2000–2001* (Ithaca, NY: Cornell University Press, 2001).

14. Barbara F. Reskin and Heidi Hartmann, eds., *Women's Work,*

Men's Work: Sex Segregation on the Job (Washington, DC: National Academy Press, 1986); Francine D. Blau and Lawrence M. Kahn, "Gender Differences in Pay," *Journal of Economic Perspectives,* Vol. 14, No. 4, Fall 2000, 75–99.

15. Blau and Kahn, "Gender Differences in Pay;" Jane Waldfogel, "Understanding the 'Family Gap' in Pay for Women with Children," *Journal of Economic Perspectives,* Vol. 12, No. 1, Winter 1998, 137–156.

16. Paul Osterman, "Employers in the Low-Wage/Low-Skill Labor Market," in Kazis and Miller, eds., *Low-Wage Workers in the New Economy.*

17. Harry J. Holzer, *What Employers Want: Job Prospects for Less-Educated Workers* (New York: Russell Sage Foundation, 1996).

18. For example, Karen Brodkin Sacks noted that the health-care industry is "so stratified by race and gender that the uniforms worn to distinguish the jobs and statuses of health-care workers are largely redundant." Karen Brodkin Sacks, "Does It Pay to Care?," in Emily K. Abel and Margaret K. Nelson, eds., *Circles of Care: Work and Identity in Women's Lives* (Albany: SUNY Press, 1990). The same kinds of stratification can be found in secretarial work, food service, hotels, and sales occupations. The service-sector workforce is highly feminized at the bottom. From 1950–1990, women filled 60 percent of all new service-sector employment and 74 percent of all new low-wage jobs. See Cameron Lynne MacDonald and Carmen Sirianni, eds., *Working in the Service Society* (Philadelphia: Temple University Press, 1996).

19. Mishel, et al., *The State of Working America 2002–2003.*

20. Vicky Lovell and Heidi Hartmann, "Increasing Economic Security for Low-Wage Women Workers," in Kazis and Miller, eds., *Low-Wage Workers in the New Economy.*

21. Joan Williams, *Unbending Gender: Why Family and Work Conflict and What to Do About It* (Oxford and New York: Oxford University Press, 2000).

22. Blau and Kahn, "Gender Differences in Pay"; Eileen Apple-

baum, Thomas Bailey, Peter Berg, and Arne Kalleberg, "Shared Work/
Valued Care: New Norms for Organizing Market Work and Unpaid
Care Work," IRRA Annual Meeting, New Orleans, January 7, 2001.

23. Blau and Kahn, "Gender Differences in Pay."

24. Anthony P. Carnevale and Stephen J. Rose, "Low Earners:
Who Are They? Do They Have a Way Out?," in Kazis and Miller, eds.,
Low-Wage Workers in the New Economy. Service and sales workers are
much more likely than less-skilled manual workers to be low earners
(68 percent to 40 percent). Conversely, fully one-third of manual
workers but only 13 percent of service and sales workers reached the
$25,000 level.

25. U.S. Census Bureau, *A Profile of the Working Poor,* 1998.

26. Jody Heymann, *The Widening Gap: Why America's Working
Families Are in Jeopardy and What Can Be Done About It* (New York:
Basic Books, 2000).

27. Barbara Stanek Kilbourne, George Farkas, Kurt Beron,
Dorothea Weir, and Paula England, "Returns to Skill, Compensating
Differentials and Gender Bias: Effects of Occupational Characteristics
on the Wages of White Women and Men," *American Journal of Soci-
ology,* Vol. 100, Issue 3, November 1994, 689–719; Blau and Kahn,
"Gender Differences in Pay." Even controlling for the measured personal characteristics of workers and a variety of characteristics of occupations, female occupations pay less. Williams, *Unbending Gender*;
Carnevale and Rose, "Low Earners."

28. Holly Sklar, Laryssa Mykyta, and Susan Wefald, *Raise the
Floor: Wages and Policies That Work For All of Us* (New York: Ms.
Foundation for Women, 2001). Female-dominated service and sales
workers are much more likely than less-skilled manual workers to be
low earners. Carnevale and Rose, "Low Earners."

29. Carnevale and Rose, "Low Earners."

30. Williams, *Unbending Gender.*

31. Looking at a five-year period between 1987 and 1992, for example, among women who started below $15,000 in 1987, 53 percent

were low earners in 1992 and another 18 percent were no longer working. To the degree they moved up, most made only the short step into the next earnings category of $15,000–$25,000; only 9 percent earned more than $25,000. Carnevale and Rose, "Low Earners."

32. *Contingent Workers: Incomes and Benefits Lag Behind Those of Rest of Workforce*, GAO Report, June 2000, GAO/HEHS-00-76; Mishel, et al., *The State of Working America, 2000–2001*.

33. Mishel, et al., *The State of Working America 1998–1999*.

34. Applebaum, et al., "Shared Work/Valued Care."

35. Ibid.

36. Lovell and Hartmann, "Increasing Economic Security for Low-Wage Women Workers."

37. Williams, *Unbending Gender*; Waldfogel, "Understanding the 'Family Gap' in Pay for Women with Children."

38. Waldfogel, "Understanding the 'Family Gap' in Pay for Women with Children"; Blau and Kahn, "Gender Differences in Pay."

39. Blau and Kahn, "Gender Differences in Pay."

40. Williams, *Unbending Gender*. Nearly two-thirds of women are not ideal workers even in the minimal sense of working forty hours a week. One-fourth are still homemakers and many more work part-time.

41. Lovell and Hartmann, "Increasing Economic Security for Low-Wage Women Workers"; Waldfogel, "Understanding the 'Family Gap' in Pay for Women with Children."

42. Williams, *Unbending Gender*. Jobs requiring extensive overtime exclude virtually all mothers.

43. Ibid.

44. Lovell and Hartmann, "Increasing Economic Security for Low-Wage Women Workers"; Heymann, *The Widening Gap*; and Waldfogel, "Understanding the 'Family Gap' in Pay for Women with Children."

45. Waldfogel, "Understanding the 'Family Gap' in Pay for

Women with Children"; see also Lovell and Hartmann, "Increasing Economic Security for Low-Wage Women Workers"; and Williams, *Unbending Gender*.

46. Waldfogel, "Understanding the 'Family Gap' in Pay for Women with Children"; and Williams, *Unbending Gender*.

47. Ibid.

48. Frank Levy, *The New Dollars and Dreams: American Incomes and Economic Change* (New York: The Russell Sage Foundation, 1998).

49. Richard W. Judy and Carol D. Amici, *Workforce 2020: Work and Workers in the 21st Century* (Indianapolis: Hudson Institute, 1997).

50. Mishel, et al., *The State of Working America 2000–2001*.

51. Judy and Amici, *Workforce 2020*.

52. Harry J. Holzer, "Career Advancement Prospects and Strategies for Low-Wage Minority Workers," in Kazis and Miller, eds., *Low-Wage Workers in the New Economy*.

53. Holzer, *What Employers Want*.

54. Cameron Lynne Macdonald and Carmen Sirianni, "The Service Society and the Changing Experience of Work," in Macdonald and Sirianni, eds., *Working in the Service Society*.

55. *Contingent Workers*, GAO Report.

56. William Julius Wilson, *When Work Disappears* (New York: Alfred A. Knopf, 1996).

57. Ibid.; Harry J. Holzer, "Mismatch in the Low-Wage Labor Market: Job Hiring Perspective," in *The Low-Wage Labor Market: Challenges and Opportunities for Economic Self-Sufficiency*, U.S. Department of Health and Human Services, Office of the Secretary, Assistant Secretary for Planning and Evaluation, Washington, DC, December, 1999.

58. Holzer, "Career Advancement Prospects and Strategies for Low-Wage Minority Workers."

59. Ibid.

60. Christopher Jencks, "Who Should Get In?," *The New York Review of Books,* November 29, 2001.

61. George J. Borjas, Richard B. Freeman, and Lawrence F. Katz, *How Much Do Immigration and Trade Affect Labor Market Outcomes?,* Brookings Papers on Economic Activity, 1:1997.

62. Michael Fix and Jeffrey S. Passel, *Immigration and Immigrants: Setting the Record Straight* (Washington, DC: The Urban Institute, 1994).

63. Sonia M. Perez and Cecilia Munoz, "Latino Low-Wage Workers: A Look at Immigrant Workers," in Kazis and Miller, eds., *Low-Wage Workers in the New Economy.*

64. Borjas, et al., *How Much Do Immigration and Trade Affect Labor Market Outcomes?*

65. Ibid.

66. D'Vera Cohen, "Illegal Residents Exceed Estimate," *The Washington Post,* March 18, 2001; Jencks, "Who Should Get In?"

67. Jencks, "Who Should Get In?"

68. Ibid.

69. James P. Smith and Barry Edmonston, eds., *The New Americans: Economic Demographics and Fiscal Effects of Immigration* (Washington, DC: National Research Council, National Academy Press, 1997); Perez and Munoz, "Latino Low-Wage Workers."

70. Smith and Edmonston, eds., *The New Americans.*

71. Ibid.

72. Steven Greenhouse, "Hispanic Workers Die at Higher Rate," *The New York Times,* July 16, 2001.

73. Ibid.

74. Jencks, "Who Should Get In?"

75. Perez and Munoz, "Latino Low-Wage Workers."

76. David Barboza, "Meatpacker's Profit Hinge on Pool of Immigrant Labor," *The New York Times,* December 21, 2001.

77. Ibid.

78. Paul Pringle, "Threadbare Existence," *Dallas Morning News,* March 3, 2000.

CHAPTER 5: HOW LOW-WAGE JOBS DAMAGE US ALL

1. Richard B. Freeman, "Is the New Income Inequality the Achilles' Heel of the American Economy?" in James A. Auerbach and Richard S. Belous, eds., *The Inequality Paradox: Growth of Income Disparity* (Washington, DC: National Policy Association, 1998), 219–233 at 224; Lawrence Mishel, Jared Bernstein, and John Schmitt, *The State of Working America 2000–2001* (Ithaca, NY: Cornell University Press, 2001).

2. Mishel, et al., *The State of Working America 2000–2001*; Freeman, "Is the New Income Inequality the Achilles' Heel of the American Economy?"; and Don Terry, "U.S. Child Poverty Rate Fell as Economy Grew, But is Above 1979 Level," *The New York Times,* August 11, 2000.

3. Freeman, "Is the New Income Inequality the Achilles' Heel of the American Economy?"; and Greg Duncan, W. Jean Yeung, Jeanne Brooks-Gunn, and Judith R. Smith, "How Much Does Childhood Poverty Affect the Life-Chances of Children?" *American Sociological Review,* June 1998, 406–424.

4. David T. Ellwood, "Winners and Losers in America: Taking the Measure of the New Economic Realities," Prepared for Aspen Institute Domestic Strategy Group Meeting, 1998.

5. Edmund S. Phelps, *Rewarding Work: How to Restore Participation and Self-Support to Free Enterprise* (Cambridge, MA: Harvard University Press, 1997), 103.

6. Alexander Stille, "Grounded by an Income Gap," *The New York Times,* December 15, 2001.

7. Sara S. McLanahan, Nan Marie Astone, and Nadine F. Marks, "The Role of Mother-Only Families in Reproducing Poverty," in Aletha C. Huston, ed., *Children in Poverty: Child Development and Public Policy* (Cambridge: Cambridge University Press, 1991), 51–78

at 68. In studies of children's early cognitive and physical development, family income in the first five years of life strongly correlates with a child's developmental outcomes in early and middle childhood. Duncan, et al., "How Much Does Childhood Poverty Affect the Life-Chances of Children?"

8. Duncan, et al., "How Much Does Childhood Poverty Affect the Life-Chances of Children?" This is true when one controls for family characteristics such as maternal schooling, household structure, and welfare receipt. Greg J. Duncan, "The Economic Environment of Childhood," in Huston, ed., *Children in Poverty.*

9. Vonnie C. McLoyd and Leon Wilson, "The Strain of Living Poor: Parenting, Social Support and Child Mental Health," in Huston, ed., *Children in Poverty,* 105–135, 107.

10. Duncan, et al., "How Much Does Childhood Poverty Affect the Life-Chances of Children?"

11. Robert Haveman and Barbara Wolfe, *Succeeding Generations: On the Effects of Investments in Children* (New York: Russell Sage Foundation, 1994), 263; McLoyd and Wilson, "The Strain of Living Poor," 106–107.

12. Arloc Sherman, *Wasting America's Future* (Boston: Beacon Press, 1994); McLoyd and Wilson, "The Strain of Living Poor," at 107; Haveman and Wolfe, *Succeeding Generations,* 259.

13. "In Early-Childhood Education and Care, Quality Counts" in "Quality Counts 2002: Building Blocks for Success," *Education Week,* Vol. 21, No. 17, January 10, 2002.

14. Lucie White, "Quality Child Care for Low-income Families," in Joel F. Handler and Lucie White, eds., *Hard Labor: Women and Work in the Post-Welfare Era* (Armonk, NY: M.E. Sharpe, 1999), 116–142 at 126; and David T. Ellwood, *The Plight of the Working Poor* Washington, DC: Brookings Institution Children's Roundtable, No. 2, November 1999.

15. Lynn Olson, "Starting Early," in "Quality Counts 2002: Building Blocks for Success," *Education Week*; and *The Future of Children:*

Caring for Infants and Toddlers, David and Lucile Packard Foundation, Vol. 11, No. 1, Spring/Summer 2001.

16. Sara Rimer, "Children of Working Poor are Day Care's Forgotten," *The New York Times,* November 25, 1997.

17. White, "Quality Child Care for Low-income Families."

18. Rimer, "Children of Working Poor are Day Care's Forgotten."

19. National Governor's Association, "Child Care and Early Education," *National Governor's Association Policy,* September 1, 2000, http://www.nga.org/Pubs/Policies? HR/hr21:asp; "In Early-Childhood Education and Care: Quality Counts"; and Jodi Wilgoren, "Quality Day Care, Early, is Tied to Achievements as an Adult," *The New York Times,* October 22, 1999, A16.

20. Susan Muenchow, executive director of the Florida Children's Forum, in Rimer, "Children of Working Poor are Day Care's Forgotten."

21. Arloc Sherman, *Poverty Matters: The Cost of Child Poverty in America,* The Children's Defense Fund, 1997; McLanahan, et al., "The Role of Mother-Only Families in Reproducing Poverty."

22. Sherman, *Wasting America's Future*; and Jonathan Kozol, *Savage Inequalities: Children in America's Schools* (New York: Crown Publishers, 1991).

23. S. Murray, W. Evans, and R. Schwab, "Education Finance Reform and the Distribution of Education Resources," *American Economic Review* 88, 789–812.

24. David Card and Alan B. Krueger, "School Resources and Student Outcomes," *Annals of the American Academy of Political and Social Science,* September 1998, Vol. 559, 39–53.

25. Gary Burtless, introduction and summary, in Gary Burtless, ed., *Does Money Matter?* (Washington, DC: Brookings Institution Press, 1996), i–42; and Sarah E. Turner, "A Comment on Poor School Funding, Child Poverty, and Mathematics Achievement," *Research News and Comment,* June–July 2000.

26. Barbara L. Wolfe, "Poverty, Children's Health, and Health

Care Utilization," Federal Reserve Bank of NY, *Economic Policy Review*, September 1999; Dennis Raphael, "From Increasing Poverty to Societal Disintegration: How Economic Inequality Affects the Health of Individuals and Communities," in Hugh Armstrong, Pat Armstrong, and David Coburn, eds., *The Political Economy of Health and Health Care in Canada* (Toronto: Oxford University Press, 2000); Aletha C. Huston, "Antecedents, Consequences and Possible Solutions for Poverty Among Children," in Huston, ed., *Children in Poverty*, 282–314 at 291; Lorraine V. Klerman, "The Health of Poor Children: Problems and Programs," in Huston, ed., *Children in Poverty*, 136–157 at 137.

27. Huston, "Antecedents, Consequences and Possible Solutions for Poverty Among Children"; Haveman and Wolfe, *Succeeding Generations*; Robin M. Wernick, Margaret E. Weigers, and Joel W. Cohen, "Children's Health Insurance, Access to Care and Health Status: New Findings," *Health Affairs*, March/April 1998; Howard B. Shapiro, "A Synopsis of Health Insurance Coverage in the United States," Presentation before the Aspen Institute Domestic Strategy Group, August 1999.

28. Wolfe, "Poverty, Children's Health, and Health Care Utilization"; Lolly Bowean, "Children Are Uninsured Because Parents Don't Know They Qualify, Report Says," *The Wall Street Journal*, August 10, 2000; Elliot K. Wicks and Jack A. Meyer, *Covering America: Real Remedies for the Uninsured*, Economic and Social Research Institute Occasional Paper, December 2001.

29. Wernick, et. al., "Children's Health Insurance, Access to Care and Health Status: New Findings."

30. Ibid.

31. Louise G. Trubek, "The Health Care Puzzle," in Handler and White, eds., *Hard Labor*, 143–151 at 150.

32. *Employee Benefits in Small Private Industry Establishments, 1996*, Bureau of Labor Statistics; *Reports on Employee Benefits in Medium and Large Private Establishments*, Bureau of Labor Statistics,

1995; James T. Bond, Ellen Galinsky, and Jennifer E. Swanberg, *The 1997 National Study of the Changing Workforce* (New York: Families and Work Institute, 1997).

33. *Employee Benefits in Small Private Industry Establishments, 1996*; and *Reports on Employee Benefits in Medium and Large Private Establishments.*

34. Jody Heymann, *The Widening Gap: Why America's Working Families Are in Jeopardy and What Can Be Done About It* (New York: Basic Books, 2000).

35. *Access Denied: Restoring the Nation's Commitment to Equal Educational Opportunity*, A Report of the Advisory Committee on Student Financial Assistance, Washington, DC, February 2001.

36. Ibid.

37. "Family Money Top Factor in College Attendance," Associated Press, August 11, 1998.

38. David T. Ellwood and Thomas J. Kane, *Who is Getting a College Education?: Family Background and the Growing Gaps in Enrollment*, Working Paper, Kennedy School of Government, February 1999.

39. Ibid.

40. National Center for Education Statistics, *Condition of Education, 1997*, 120. The premium for some college education has also increased over this same period. See National Center for Education Statistics, *Condition of Education*, 1997.

41. Ellwood, "Winners and Losers in America."

42. Ibid.

43. Ellwood and Kane, *Who is Getting a College Education?*

44. Albert B. Crenshaw, "College Hopes Dim for the Poor," *The Washington Post*, February 25, 2001.

45. *Access Denied.*

46. Sherman, *Poverty Matters*; Deborah A. Phillips, "With a Little Help: Children in Poverty and Child Care," in Huston, ed., *Children in Poverty*.

47. Phillips, "With a Little Help"; National Governor's Association, "Child Care and Early Education," *National Governor's Association Policy.*

48. Dale Russakoff, "Cut Out of Prosperity, Cutting Out at the Polls," *The Washington Post,* October 24, 2000; Committee for the Study of the American Electorate, August 30, 2001; Stille, "Grounded by an Income Gap."

49. Rick Bragg, "In a Working-Poor Town, Candidates Are Dismissed as Being Out of Touch," *The New York Times,* September 17, 2000; Russakoff, "Cut Out of Prosperity, Cutting Out at the Polls"; Committee for the Study of the American Electorate, August 30, 2001.

50. Stille, "Grounded by an Income Gap."

51. Randall J. Olsen and George Farkas, "The Effect of Economic Opportunity and Family Background on Adolescent Cohabitation and Childbearing Among Low-Income Blacks," *Journal of Labor Economics,* 1990, Vol. 8, No. 3, 341–62.

52. Ellwood, "Winners and Losers in America."

53. Virginia Knox, Cynthia Miller, and Lisa A. Gennetian, *Reforming Welfare and Rewarding Work: A Summary of the Final Report on the Minnesota Family Investment Program,* Manpower Demonstration Research Corporation, 2000.

54. Kathryn M. Neckerman, Robert Aponte, and William Julius Wilson, "Family Structure, Black Unemployment and American Social Policy," in Margaret Weir, Ann Shola Orloff, and Theda Skocpol, eds., *The Politics of Social Policy in the United States* (Princeton: Princeton University Press, 1988); William Julius Wilson, *The Truly Disadvantaged* (Chicago: University of Chicago Press, 1987); Greg J. Duncan, Johanne Borsjoly, and Timothy Smeeding, "Economic Mobility of Young Workers in the 1970s and 1980s," *Demography,* November 1996, Vol. 33, No. 4, 497–509.

55. Shelly Lundberg and Robert D. Plotnick, "Adolescent Premarital Childbearing: Do Economic Incentives Matter?" *Journal of Labor Economics,* Vol. 13, No. 2, April 1995, 177–200.

56. Phelps, *Rewarding Work*.

57. Frank Furstenberg, Jr., "As the Pendulum Swings: Teenage-Childbearing and Social Concern," *Family Relations*, Vol. 40, No. 2, 136, April 1991.

58. Mishel, et al., *The State of Working America 2000–2001*.

59. Peter Phillips, *A Living Wage Makes Good Economic Sense for Local Communities*, www.commondreams.org, December 7, 2001.

60. Holly Sklar, Laryssa Mykyta, and Susan Wefald, *Raise the Floor: Wages and Policies That Work for All of Us* (New York: Ms. Foundation for Women, 2001).

61. Phelps, *Rewarding Work*.

62. Jared Bernstein and Ellen Houston, *Crime and Work: What We Can Learn From the Low-Wage Labor Market*, Economic Policy Institute, Washington, DC, 2000; Richard B. Freeman and William M. Rodgers III, "Area Economic Conditions and the Labor Market Outcomes of Young Men in the 1990s Expansion," NBER Working Paper 7073, 1999; Richard B. Freeman, "Does the Booming Economy Help Explain the Fall in Crime?" NBER and Centre for Economic Performance, LSE, February 2000; Gene Carats, "Rising Wages, Safer Streets: One Reason Crime is Dropping," *Business Week*, June 21, 1999, quoting Jeff Grogger, *Journal of Labor Economics*.

63. Bernstein and Houston, *Crime and Work*.

64. Richard B. Freeman, "Why Do So Many Young American Men Commit Crimes and What Might We Do About It," *Journal of Economic Perspectives*, Vol. 10, No. 1, Winter 1996, 25–42 at 40.

65. Ibid.

66. Ibid.

67. Freeman, "Is the New Inequality the Achilles' Heel of the American Economy?"

68. Stille, "Grounded by an Income Gap."

69. Byrne Armiento, *The Business Case for Employer Investment in Low-Wage Workers*, Families and Work Institute, June 1999; Bond, et al., *The 1997 National Study of the Changing Workforce*, 13.

70. Harry Holzer, "Job Change and Job Stability Among Less-Skilled Workers"; Linda Datcher-Loury and Glenn Loury, "The Effect of Attitudes and Aspirations on the Labor Supply of Young Men," in Richard B. Freeman and Harry J. Holzer, eds., *The Black Youth Employment Crisis* (Chicago: University of Chicago Press, 1986). Black youths who think of themselves as moving on to higher-level jobs accept and hold the jobs that are available to them as youths, whereas black youths who think they will remain in those jobs permanently have a much weaker attachment to them; Lynn Wagner, *Provider*, May 1998.

71. Armiento, *The Business Case for Employer Investment in Low-Wage Workers.*

72. *Economic Report of the President* (Washington, DC: U.S. Government Printing Office, 2003), 276.

73. Armiento, *The Business Case for Employer Investment in Low-Wage Workers.*

74. Frank Levy, *The New Dollars and Dreams: American Incomes and Economic Change* (New York: Russell Sage Foundation, 1998).

75. Alan B. Kreuger, "Economic Scene: A Small Dose of Common Sense Would Help Congress Break the Gridlock over Airport Security," *The New York Times*, November 15, 2001.

76. Michael Reich, Peter Hall, and Ken Jacobs, *Living Wages and Airport Security, Preliminary Report*, Institute for Labor and Employment, University of California, September 20, 2001; Susan C. Eaton, *Pennsylvania's Nursing Homes: Promoting Quality Care and Quality Jobs*, Keystone Research Center High Road Industry Series, #1, April 1997; Marcy Whitebook, Carollee Howes, and Deborah Phillips, *Worthy Work, Unlivable Wages: The National Child Care Staffing Study, 1988–1997*, Center for the Child Care Workforce, Washington, DC, 1998.

77. Reich, et al., *Living Wages and Airport Security, Preliminary Report.*

78. Eaton, *Pennsylvania's Nursing Homes*; Whitebook, et al., *Worthy Work, Unlivable Wages*; Whitebook, "Child Care Workers: High Demand, Low Wages," *Annals of the American Academy of Political and Social Science,* May 1999; SEIU Report on Nursing Homes.

79. Susan Levine, "Care at Maryland Nursing Homes," *The Washington Post,* January 9, 2000.

80. Ibid.

81. Ibid.

82. Institute of Medicine, Committee on Nursing Home Regulation, *Improving the Quality of Care in Nursing Homes* (Washington, DC: National Academy Press, 1986); Rosalie A. Kane and R.L. Kane, *Long-Term Care: Principles, Programs and Policies* (New York: Springer Publishing Company, 1987); Mary Ann Wilner and Ann Wyatt, *Paraprofessionals on the Front Lines: Improving Their Jobs— Improving the Quality of Long-term Care,* A Conference Background Paper Prepared for the AARP Long-Term Care Initiative, September 1998.

83. Steven L. Dawson, *Direct-Care Health Workers: The Unnecessary Crisis in Long-Term Care* (New York: Healthcare Paraprofessional Institute, 2000).

84. Peter Pitegoff, "Shaping Regional Economies to Sustain Quality Work," in Handler and White, eds, *Hard Labor.*

85. Sara Rimer, "Home Aides for the Frail Elderly in Short Supply," *The New York Times,* January 3, 2000; Dawson, *Direct-Care Health Workers.*

86. R.A. Kane, "Toward Competent, Caring Paid Caregivers," *The Gerontologist,* Vol. 29, No. 3, 1989.

87. Interview with Artie Nathan, vice president, human resources, Mirage Hotels International.

88. Armiento, *The Business Case for Employer Investment in Low-Wage Workers.*

89. Norman Daniels, Bruce Kennedy, and Ichiro Kawachi, "Justice is Good for Our Health," *Boston Review,* February/March 2000.

90. Richard G. Wilkinson, "Why is Inequality Bad for Health?" in James A. Auerbach and Barbara Kivimae Krimgold, eds., *Income, Socioeconomic Status and Health: Exploring the Relationships*, National Policy Association and Academy for Health Services Research and Health Policy, 2001; Sheryl Gay Stalber, "Poor People are Fighting Baffling Surge in Asthma," *The New York Times*, October 18, 1999.

91. Daniels, et al., "Justice is Good for Our Health."

92. Ibid.; Raphael, "From Increasing Poverty to Societal Disintegration: How Economic Inequality Affects the Health of Individuals and Communities," in Armstrong, et al., eds., *The Political Economy of Health and Health Care in Canada*; James Lardner, "Americans Widening Gap in Incomes May Be Narrowing Our Life Spans," *The Washington Post*, August 16, 1998.

93. J.R. Kaplan, E. Pamuk, J.W. Lynch, J.W. Cohen, and J.L. Balfou, "Income Inequality and Mortality in the U.S.," *British Medical Journal* 312, 999–1003; Ichiro Kawachi and Bruce P. Kennedy, "How Income Inequality Affects Health: Evidence from Research in the United States," in Auerbach and Krimgold, eds., *Income, Socioeconomic Status and Health*; Wilkinson, "Why is Inequality Bad for Health?"; Raphael, "From Increasing Poverty to Societal Disintegration."

94. Kawachi and Kennedy, "How Income Inequality Affects Health."

95. Ibid.; Daniels, et al., "Justice is Good for Our Health."

96. Wilkinson, "Why is Inequality Bad for Health?"

CHAPTER 6: AN APOLOGY FOR INDIFFERENCE

1. Richard B. Freeman, *When Earnings Diverge: Causes, Consequences, and Cures for the New Inequality in the U.S.*, Washington DC, National Policy Association Report #284, 1997.

2. Peter Gottschalk, "Inequality, Income Growth, and Mobility: The Basic Facts," *Journal of Economic Perspectives*, Vol. 11, No. 1, Spring 1997, 21–40.

3. They looked at the years from 1968 to 1993. Peter Gottschalk

and Sheldon Danziger, "Family Income Mobility—How Much is There, and Has It Changed?" in James A. Auerbach and Richard Belous, eds., *The Inequality Paradox: Growth of Income Disparity Inequality* (Washington, DC: National Policy Association, 1998). Other mobility studies found similar results. See Paul Osterman, *Securing Prosperity: How the American Labor Market Has Changed and What to Do about It* (Princeton: Princeton University Press, 1999) in which he found that 49.2 percent of men who were in the bottom-earnings quintile in 1979 remained in that quintile in 1995. See also Daniel McMurrer, Mark Condon, and Isabel Sawhill, *International Mobility in the United States* (Washington, DC: The Urban Institute, 1997) where they found that between 1979 and 1986 less than half moved out of the bottom quintile during that period.

4. Annette Bernhardt, Martina Morris, Mark S. Handcock, and Marc A. Scott, *Divergent Paths: Economic Mobility in the New American Labor Market* (New York: Russell Sage Foundation, 2001).

5. Ibid.; Annette Bernhardt, Martina Morris, Mark S. Handcock, and Marc A. Scott, *Summary of Findings: Work and Opportunity in the Post-Industrial Labor Market,* Institute on Education and the Economy, IEE Working Paper No. 6, February 1995; Thomas Bailey and Annette Bernhardt, "In Search of the High Road in a Low-Wage Industry," *Politics and Society,* Vol. 25, No. 2, June 1997, 179–201.

6. Bernhardt, et al., *Divergent Paths*; Bernhardt, et al., *Summary of Findings.* In the telecommunications industry, long-distance products were stratified according to customers. For high-revenue customers, workers are trained to address many issues and spend a considerable amount of time with each client. For low-revenue customers, workers provide a small number of services to a large number of customers, yet receive training in a limited number of tasks. See Rosemary Batt, "Explaining Wage Inequality in Telecommunications Services: Customer Segmentation, Human Resource Practices, and Union Decline. The Role of Business Strategy and Human Resource Practices," *Industrial and Labor Relations Review* 54(2,A), 2001, 425–49.

7. Bernhardt, et al., *Divergent Paths.*

8. Greg J. Duncan, Johanne Boisjoly, and Timothy Smeeding, "Economic Mobility of Young Workers in the 1970s and 1980s," *Demography,* November 1996.

9. Gottschalk and Danziger, "Family Income Mobility—How Much is There and Has It Changed?"; Lawrence Mishel, Jared Bernstein, and John Schmitt, *The State of Working America 2000–2001* (Ithaca, NY: Cornell University Press, 2001).

10. The United States had the lowest share of workers in the bottom fifth of the labor market moving on to the second fifth of earners and the lowest share moving into the top 60 percent of wage earners. Mishel, et al., *The State of Working America 2000–2001.*

11. Bernhardt, et al., *Divergent Paths.*

12. Bernhardt, et al., *Summary of Findings.*

13. David R. Howell and Susan S. Wieler, "Skill-Biased Demand Shifts and the Collapse in the United States: A Critical Perspective," *Eastern Economic Journal,* Summer 1998; Michael J. Handel, "Is There a Skills Crisis? Trends in Job Skill Requirements, Technology, and Wage Inequality in the United States," The Jerome Levy Economics Institute of Bard College, Public Policy Brief, No. 62, 2000. This article cites the many skills mismatch theories. David M. Gordon, *Fat and Mean* (New York: The Free Press, 1996).

14. Robert B. Reich, "Jobs: Skills Before Credentials," *Training,* April 1994.

15. Handel, "Is There a Skills Crisis?" Richard Rothstein, "Calculus for Waitresses? A 'New Economy' Myth," *The New York Times,* October 27, 1999.

16. George T. Silvestri, "Employment Outlook: 1996–2008: Occupational Employment Projections to 2006," *Monthly Labor Review,* November 1997. Jobs requiring only short-term on-the-job training—training in which workers can learn the basic job skills in a few weeks—constitute the largest education and training category. See

also *Report on the American Workforce,* "Overview of Report on the American Workforce 1999," U.S. Department of Labor.

17. Silvestri, "Employment Outlook: 1996–2008."

18. Colin Crouch, David Finegold, and Mair Sako, *Are Skills the Answer? The Political Economy of Skill Creation in Advanced Industrial Countries* (New York: Oxford University Press, 1999); Anthony P. Carnevale and Donna M. Desrochers, "Employer Training: The High Road, the Low Road and the Muddy Middle Path," in Ray Marshall, ed., *Restoring Broadly Shared Prosperity* (Washington, DC: Economic Policy Institute, 1997).

19. Linda Barrington, The Conference Board, "Does a Rising Tide Lift All Boats? America's Full-Time Working Poor Reap Limited Gains in the New Economy," Conference Report 1271-00-RR.

20. Ibid.

21. Daniel E. Hecker, "Employment Outlook: 2000–2010: Occupational Employment Projections to 2010," *Monthly Labor Review,* November 2001.

22. Ibid.; Rothstein, "Calculus for Waitresses? A 'New Economy' Myth."

23. Richard W. Judy and Carol D'Amico, *Workforce 2020: Work and Workers in the 21st Century* (Indianapolis: Hudson Institute, 1997).

24. Hecker, "Employment Outlook: 2000–2010."

25. Ibid.

26. Crouch, et al., *Are Skills the Answer?*

27. Ibid.

28. Mishel, et al., *The State of Working America 2000–2001.*

29. Harry J. Holzer, *What Employers Want: Job Prospects for Less-Educated Workers* (New York: Russell Sage Foundation, 1996).

30. Ibid.

31. And once a person leaves the educational system, training is generally provided by work. Amanda Ahlstrand, Max Armbruster, Laurie Bassi, Dan McMurrer, and Mark Van Buren, "Workplace Edu-

cation Investments and Strategies for Lower-Wage Workers: Patterns and Practices in Employer-Provided Education in the United States," in Richard Kazis and Mark Miller, *Low-Wage Workers in the New Economy* (Washington, DC: Urban Institute Press, 2001).

32. Ibid.

33. *Economic Report of the President*, U.S. Government Printing Office, Washington, DC, 2001, 395; Richard Freeman, "Are Your Wages Set in Beijing?," *Journal of Economic Perspectives*, Vol. 9, No. 3, Summer 1995, 15–32; Mishel, et al., *The State of Working America 2000–2001*.

34. Mishel, et al., *The State of Working America 2000–2001*.

35. See Adrian Wood, "How Trade Hurt Unskilled Workers," *Journal of Economic Perspectives*, Vol. 9, No. 3, Summer 1995, 57–80; Adrian Wood, *North-South Trade, Employment and Inequality: Changing Fortunes in a Skill-Driven World* (Oxford: Clarendon Press, 1994); Edward E. Leamer, "Trade, Wages and Revolving-Door Ideas," Working Paper No. 4716, National Bureau of Economic Research, Cambridge, 1994; Edward E. Leamer, "A Trade Economist's View of U.S. Wages and 'Globalization,'" paper prepared for a Brookings Institution conference on imports, exports and the American worker, mimeo, Anderson Graduate School of Management, University of California at Los Angeles, February 1995; Paul Krugman and Robert Z. Lawrence, "Trade, Jobs, and Wages," *Scientific American*, April 1994, 270:4 44–49; George Borjas, Richard Freeman, and Lawrence Katz, "On the Labor Market Effects of Immigration and Trade," in George Borjas and Richard Freeman, eds., *Immigration and the Work Force* (Chicago: University of Chicago Press and NBER, 1992), 213–44; Ravi Batra, *The Myth of Free Trade* (New York: Charles Scribner's Sons, 1993); Robert Z. Lawrence and Matthew J. Slaughter, "International Trade and American Wages in the 1980s: Giant Sucking Sound or Small Hiccup," Brookings Papers on Economic Activity, 2, 1993, 161–226; J. David Richardson, "Income Inequality and Trade: How to Think, What to Conclude," *Journal of Economic Perspectives*,

Vol. 9, No. 3, Summer 1995, 33–55; Freeman, "Are Your Wages Set in Beijing?"; Gary Burtless, Robert Z. Lawrence, Robert E. Litan, and Robert J. Shapiro, *Globaphobia: Confronting Fears About Open Trade* (Washington, DC: Brookings Institution, Progressive Policy Institute, Twentieth Century Fund, 1998); Stephen A. Herzenberg, John A. Alic, and Howard Wial, *New Rules for a New Economy: Employment and Opportunity in Postindustrial America* (Ithaca, NY: Cornell University Press, 1998); William Greider, *One World, Ready or Not: The Manic Logic of Global Capitalism* (New York: Simon and Schuster, 1997); Mishel, et al., *The State of Working America 2000–2001*; Robert Kuttner, *Everything for Sale: The Virtues and Limits of Markets* (New York: Alfred A. Knopf, 1997); Ethan B. Kapstein, "Workers and the World Economy," *Foreign Affairs*, May/June, 1996, 16–37; Alan Tonelson, *The Race to the Bottom: Why a Worldwide Worker Surplus and Uncontrolled Free Trade are Sinking American Living Standards* (Boulder, CO: Westview Press, 2000).

36. Burtless, et al., *Globaphobia*.

37. Mishel, et al., *The State of Working America 2000–2001*.

38. Ibid.; Freeman, "Are Your Wages Set in Beijing?"

39. Herzenberg, et al., *New Rules for a New Economy*.

40. Beth Shulman, "Yes, Union," *The American Prospect,* November–December 1996; Freeman, "Are Your Wages Set in Beijing?"; Burtless, et al., *Globaphobia*.

41. Freeman, "Are Your Wages Set in Beijing?"; Mishel, et al., *The State of Working America 2000–2001*.

42. Aaron Bernstein, "Backlash: Behind the Anxiety Over Globalization," *Business Week*, April 24, 2000.

43. Freeman, "Are Your Wages Set in Beijing?"; Burtless, et al., *Globaphobia*; Herzenberg, et al., *New Rules for a New Economy*.

44. Paul Krugman, "We Are Not the World," *The New York Times*, February 13, 1997.

45. Ibid.

46. Richard Freeman, "The Facts About Rising Economic Dispar-

ity," in Auerbach and Belous, eds., *The Inequality Paradox*; Timothy M. Smeeding, "U.S. Income Inequality in a Cross-National Perspective: Why Are We So Different?" in Auerbach and Belous, eds., *The Inequality Paradox*; Freeman, "Are Your Wages Set in Beijing?"

47. Smeeding, "U.S. Income Inequality in a Cross-National Perspective."

48. Burtless, et al., *Globaphobia*, 114.

49. "Shaping Globalization After Seattle," *ILO Focus*, Spring 2000, 3.

50. Dani Rodrick, "Whose Trade," *The Nation*, December 6, 1999.

51. Krugman, "We Are Not the World."

52. Even President Clinton embraced the role of faith-based organizations, but saw them as working with government, rather than as a substitute for such programs. See E.J. Dionne, Jr. and John D. Iulio, Jr., eds., *What's God Got To Do With the American Experiment?* (Washington, DC: Brookings Institution Press, 2000).

53. Associated Press, "Working Poor Descend on Food Banks, Other Relief Agencies," CNN.com, December 13, 2000.

54. Ibid.

55. Arloc Sherman, *Poverty Matters: The Cost of Child Poverty in America*, The Children's Defense Fund, 1997.

CHAPTER 7: A QUESTION OF POWER

1. Leonard Silk and Mark Silk, *Making Capitalism Work* (New York: New York University Press, 1996).

2. James K. Galbraith, *Created Unequal: The Crisis in American Pay* (New York: The Free Press, 1998), 10.

3. Nicole M. Fortin and Thomas Lemieux, "Institutional Changes and Rising Wage Inequality: Is There a Linkage?," *Journal of Economic Perspectives*, Vol. 11, No. 2, Spring 1997, 75–96.

4. Alan Brinkley, *The End of Reform* (New York: Alfred A. Knopf, 1995).

5. Robert H. Zieger, *American Workers, American Unions* (Baltimore: Johns Hopkins University Press, 1994).

6. Peter Cappelli, et al., *Change at Work* (New York: Oxford University Press, 1997).

7. The large size of many of the firms allowed them to efficiently purchase health insurance and create pension reserves for their employees, which would supplement their Social Security. Paul Osterman, Thomas Kochan, Richard Locke, and Michael Piore, *Draft of the Task Force on Reconstructing America's Labor Market Institutions, A Report of a Project Supported by the Ford and Rockefeller Foundations*, Institute for Work and Employment Research, Massachusetts Institute of Technology, Sloan School of Management, August 2000.

8. Katherine V.W. Stone, "The New Psychological Contract: Implications of the Changing Workplace for Labor and Employment Law," 48 *UCLA Law Review* 519, February 2001; Osterman, et al., *Draft of the Task Force on Reconstructing America's Labor Market Institutions.*

9. Fortin and Lemieux, "Institutional Changes and Rising Wage Inequality."

10. George Borjas, Richard B. Freeman, and Lawrence F. Katz, *How Much Do Immigration and Trade Affect Labor Market Outcomes?*, Brooking Papers on Economic Activity, 1, 1997; Lawrence Mishel, Jared Bernstein, and John Schmitt, *The State of Working America 2000–2001* (Ithaca, NY: Cornell University Press, 2001).

11. Mishel, et al., *The State of Working America 2000–2001.*

12. Aaron Bernstein, "Backlash: Behind the Anxiety Over Globalization," *Business Week*, April 24, 2000.

13. Mishel, et al., *The State of Working America 2000–2001.* In the eighties, General Electric began moving their appliance factories to Mexico. Employers threatened that they would close their plant or move to lower-wage locations if their workers refused to accept reduced wage and benefit packages in order to compete with cheaper

imports. With the visible experience of employers moving production offshore, GE workers were fearful of losing their jobs. These threats of relocation or plant closure forced workers to grant wage and benefit concessions in the remaining plants.

14. Kate Bronfenbrenner, *Final Report: The Effects of Plant Closing or Threat of Plant Closing on the Right of Workers to Organize,* Submitted to the Labor Secretariat of the North American Commission for Labor Cooperation, September 30, 1996.

15. Ibid.

16. Ibid.

17. Ibid.

18. Ibid. As discussed later in this chapter, these same threats occur when workers try to bargain for a first contract after they have overcome the obstacles and have succeeded in organizing a union to represent their interests.

19. Mishel, et al., *The State of Working America 2000–2001.* Some experts estimate that this immigration increased the relative supply of workers with less than a high school degree by 15 percent—30 percent over the 1980–95 period. See Borjas, et al., *How Much Do Immigration and Trade Affect Labor Market Outcomes?*

20. Borjas, et al., *How Much Do Immigration and Trade Affect Labor Market Outcomes?* This does not take into account the effect of an estimated eight million undocumented workers, many of whom have minimal education.

21. Ibid.; Gary Burtless, Robert Z. Lawrence, Robert E. Litan, and Robert J. Shapiro, *Globaphobia: Confronting Fears About Open Trade* (Washington, DC: Brookings Institution, Progressive Policy Institute, Twentieth Century Fund, 1998).

22. Mishel, et al., *The State of Working America 2000–2001.*

23. James Peoples, "Deregulation and the Labor Market," *Journal of Economic Perspectives,* Vol. 12, No. 3, Summer 1998, 111–130.

24. Ibid.

25. Osterman, et al., *Draft of the Task Force on Reconstructing*

America's Labor Market Institutions; Michael Belzer, *Sweatshops on Wheels* (Ann Arbor: University of Michigan, 2000).

26. Galbraith, *Created Unequal.*

27. Ibid.

28. Ibid., 266.

29. Osterman, et al., *Draft of the Task Force on Reconstructing America's Labor Market Institutions*; Belzer, *Sweatshops on Wheels.*

30. Larry W. Hunter, Annette Bernhardt, Katherine L. Hughes, and Eva Skuratowicz, "It's Not Just the ATMs: Technology, Firm Strategies, Jobs and Earnings in Retail Banking," *Industrial and Labor Relations Review* 54(2,A): 2001, 402–24; Annette Bernhardt, Martina Morris, Mark S. Handcock, and Marc A. Scott, *Divergent Paths: Economic Mobility in the New American Labor Market* (New York: Russell Sage Foundation, 2001).

31. Ernie Englander and Allen Kaufman, "The End of Managerial Ideology: From Corporate Social Responsibility to Corporate Social Indifference," working paper, GW Law School International Institute on Corporate Governance Accountability, 2003.

32. Cappelli, et al., *Change at Work.*

33. This ideological shift was best reflected in the policy statements of the Business Roundtable. Created in the mid-seventies, the Roundtable then represented nearly 200 of the largest corporations in the United States. In 1981 the Roundtable issued a statement on corporate responsibility in which it laid out a stakeholder model of the corporation—one in which the firm's responsibility was to balance the interests of employees, customers, shareholders, suppliers, government, and society in general. It recognized the "social contract" with employees that spelled out the firm's responsibilities to its workers who, in return, would work diligently and productively for the company.

But in 1996 the Business Roundtable's publication *World in Change* outlined management's new perspective on stakeholder responsibilities. In direct contrast to the 1981 statement, it reneged on its obligations to its workers. In 1997 the Roundtable more explicitly explained its revised view of the corporate role in American society and concluded that "the paramount duty of management and of boards of directors is to the corporation's stockholders; the interests of other stakeholders are relevant as a derivative of the duty to stockholders."

A shift in the form of executive compensation gave CEOs a direct self-interest in focusing on increasing stock prices over other stakeholder interests. Beginning in the mid-eighties and accelerating throughout the nineties, a growing share of executive compensation took the form of stock options. These stock options were supposed to realign the interests of CEO and other top management with those of shareholders. With the ease of buying and selling these stock options, it was in their interest to focus their efforts on enhancing share price. This realignment of executive compensation gave corporate heads even further incentives to pursue interests antithetical to those of their workers. This incentive system has been harmful not only to workers, but to all of the corporate stakeholders. See the Business Roundtable, *World in Change*, April 1996, and *Statement on Corporate Governance*, September 1997, 3. Englander and Kaufman, "The End of Managerial Ideology."

34. Frank Levy, *The New Dollars and Dreams: American Incomes and Economic Change* (New York: The Russell Sage Foundation, 1998), 189.

35. Beth Shulman, "Yes, Union," *The American Prospect*, November–December 1996.

36. Fortin and Lemieux, "Institutional Changes and Rising Wage Inequality."

37. Mishel, et al., *The State of Working America 2000–2001*; David Card, "Falling Union Membership and Rising Wage Inequality: What's the Connection," Working Paper 6520, NBER, August 2000.

38. Zieger, *American Workers, American Unions*.

39. Fortin and Lemieux, "Institutional Changes and Rising Wage Inequality."

40. Thomas A. Kochan, "The American Corporation as an Employer: Past, Present and Future Possibilities," in Carl Kaysen, ed., *The American Corporation Today* (New York: Oxford University Press, 1996), 250; Fortin and Lemieux, "Institutional Changes and Rising Wage Inequality."

41. Kochan, "The American Corporation as an Employer."

42. Thomas Byrne Edsall, "The Changing Shape of Power: A Realignment in Public Policy," in Steve Fraser and Gary Gerstle, eds., *The Rise and Fall of the New Deal Order 1930–1980* (Princeton: Princeton University Press, 1989).

43. Edsall, "The Changing Shape of Power."

44. Theodore St. Antoine, "Federal Regulation of the Workplace in the Next Century," *Chicago Kent Law Review* 631(1985), 639.

45. Thomas A. Kochan, "Back to Basics: Creating the Analytical Foundations for the Next Industrial System," *Proceedings of the Fifteenth Annual Meeting*, IRRA Series, Vol. 1, January 3–5, 1998, 237; Richard B. Freeman and Joel Rogers, *What Do Workers Want? Voice, Representation and Power in the American Workplace*, January 1998 NBER; Kochan, "The American Corporation as an Employer."

46. Kochan, "The American Corporation as an Employer," 251; Kochan, "Reconstructing the Social Contract in Employment Relations," paper prepared for conference "On Restoring Broadly Shared Economic Prosperity," Washington, DC, May 22–23, 1997.

47. Lance Compa, *Unfair Advantage: Workers Freedom of Association in the United States Under International Human Rights Standards* (New York: Human Rights Watch, 2000).

48. *Fact-Finding Report of the Commission of the Future of Worker-Management Relations* (Washington, DC: U.S. Departments of Labor and Commerce, 1994).

49. Compa, *Unfair Advantage*.

50. Paul Weiler, "Promises to Keep: Securing Workers' Right to Self-Organization Under the NLRA," 96 *Harvard Law Review* 1769, 1779–80 (1983).

51. Kochan, "Reconstructing the Social Contract in Employment Relations." See also Richard W. Hurd, *Assault on Workers' Rights,* report for the U.S. Department of Labor and U.S. Department of Commerce, Commission on the Future of Labor-Managament Relations, 1994, in which after citing more than 100 recent cases of flagrant labor violations, concluded that "the right to an independent voice for workers has become a mirage."

52. Aaron Bernstein, "Why America Needs Unions But Not the Kind They Have Now," *Business Week,* May 23, 1994, 70.

53. Kochan, "Reconstructing the Social Contract in Employment Relations."

54. Hurd, *Assault on Workers Rights.*

55. Compa, *Unfair Advantage.*

56. Ibid. See *Unfair Advantage* for a variety of cases involving egregious violations of worker rights.

57. Kochan, "The American Corporation as an Employer"; *Fact-Finding Report of the Commission on the Future of Worker-Management Relations;* Kochan, "Reconstructing the Social Contract in Employment Relations."

58. Compa, *Unfair Advantage.*

59. Zieger, *American Workers, American Unions.*

60. Kochan, "The American Corporation as an Employer," 250.

61. Bronfenbrenner, *Final Report.*

62. Card, "Falling Union Membership and Rising Wage Inequality."

63. Ibid. Mishel, et al., *The State of Working America 2000–2001.*

64. Dale Belman and John S. Heywood, "Direct and Indirect Effects of Unionization and Government Employment on Fringe Benefit Provision," *Journal of Labor Research,* Vol. 12, No. 2, Spring 1991, 111–22; Augustin Kwasi Fosu, "Nonwage Benefits as a Limited-Dependent Variable: Implications for the Impact of Unions," *Journal of Labor Research,* Vol. 14, No. 1, Winter 1993, 29–43.

65. William J. Wiatrowski, "Who Really has Access to Employer-Provided Health Benefits?" *Monthly Labor Review*, June 1995.

66. Belman and Heywood, "Direct and Indirect Effects of Unionization and Government Employment on Fringe Benefit Provision"; Fosu, "Nonwage Benefits as a Limited-Dependent Variable"; Richard B. Freeman, "The Effect of Unionism on Worker Attachment to Firms," *Journal of Labor Research*, Vol. 1, No 1, Spring 1980, 29–61.

67. *Unemployment Insurance: Role as Safety Net for Low-Wage Workers is Limited*, U.S. *General Accounting Office Report to Congressional Requestors*, GAO December 2000, GAO-01-181.

68. John W. Budd and Brian P. McCall, "The Effect of Unions on the Receipt of Unemployment Insurance Benefits," Industrial Relations Center Working Paper Series, Paper No. 94-08 (August 1994).

69. John Di Nardo and Thomas Lemieux, "Diverging Male Wage Inequality in the United States and Canada, 1981–1988: Do Institutions Explain the Difference?," *Industrial and Labor Relations Review*, Vol. 50, No. 4, July 1997; Freeman and Rogers, *What Do Workers Want?*

70. Cappelli, et al., *Change at Work*, 62.

71. Edsall, "The Changing Shape of Power."

72. Shulman, "Yes, Union."

73. Ibid.

74. Mishel, et al., *The State of Working America 2000–2001*; Paul Ryscavage, *Inequality in America: An Analysis of Trends* (Armonk, NY: M.E. Sharpe, 1999).

75. Fortin and Lemieux, "Institutional Changes and Rising Wage Inequality."

76. *Business Week*, July 17, 2000.

77. Oren M. Levin-Waldman, *Do Institutions Affect the Wage Structure: Right-to-Work Laws, Unionization, and the Minimum Wage?*, Jerome Levy Economics Institute of Bard College, No. 57,

1999; William E. Spriggs and Bruce W. Klein, *Raising the Floor: The Effects of the Minimum Wage on Low-Wage Workers* (Washington DC: Economic Policy Institute, 1994).

78. Mishel, et al., *The State of Working America 2000–2001.*

79. Fortin and Lemieux, "Institutional Changes and Rising Wage Inequality."

80. Paul Osterman, *Securing Prosperity* (Princeton: Princeton University Press, 1999), 125; Sheldon Danziger and Peter Gottschalk, *America Unequal* (Cambridge, MA: Harvard University Press, 1995).

81. Osterman, *Securing Prosperity*, 125.

82. *Unemployment Insurance.*

83. Ibid.

84. Eric Schlosser, *Fast Food Nation* (Boston: Houghton Miffin 2001).

85. Bureau of Labor Statistics, U.S. Department of Labor, *Occupational Outlook Handbook, 2002–2003 Edition* at http://www.bls.gov/oco/0005219.htm.

86. Fortin and Lemieux, "Institutional Changes and Rising Wage Inequality"; Richard B. Freeman and Lawrence Katz, *Differences and Changes in Wage Structure* (Chicago: University of Chicago Press, 1995); Galbraith, *Created Unequal.*

87. Freeman and Katz, *Differences and Changes in Wage Structure.*

88. Ryscavage, *Inequality in America*, 171; Fortin and Lemieux, "Institutional Changes and Rising Wage Inequality"; Di Nardo and Lemieux, "Diverging Male Wage Inequality in the United States and Canada, 1981–1988"; Freeman and Katz, *Differences and Changes in Wage Structure.*

89. C. Jeffrey Waddoups, "Unions and Wages In Nevada's Hotel-Casino Industry," forthcoming in *Journal of Labor Relations.*

90. Christopher W. Erickson, Catherine L. Fisk, Ruth Milkman, Daniel J.B. Mitchell, and Kent Wong, "Justice for Janitors in Los Angeles: Lessons from Three Rounds of Negotiations," *British Journal of Industrial Relations*, Vol. 41, No. 3, September 2002, 543–567.

91. In Baltimore, janitors' wages increased from $5.15 an hour to $8.00 with employer-provided health insurance.

92. ACORN (Association of Community Organizations for Reform Now) Living Wage Successes: A Compilation of Living Wage Policies on the Books (http://www.livingwagecampaign.org/victories.php). Living-wage ordinances are quite varied. In Los Angeles, the non-supervisory workers of service contractors are covered while those who provide goods under a city contract are not. Only janitors, security guards, and parking lot attendants are covered under Portland's living-wage ordinance.

93. William Greider, a leading commentator on global trade, recommends that we approve national legislation that requires firms to disclose information that would enable citizens here and abroad to determine whether corporations are adhering to these core labor standards. All U.S. multinationals would be required to identify the names and addresses of offshore factories and their subcontractor plants, the owners, and principal investors. At each facility, they would certify the existence of "core labor rights" or explain why there should be an exemption granted. It would also give Americans standing to sue if the corporation falsifies their reports to the U.S. government. Violations of these human rights would be well-publicized to ensure that consumers could make informed choices. Congress has imposed rules on multinationals before. In 1977, Congress passed the Foreign Corrupt Practices Act, which prohibits corporate bribery in overseas projects. See William Greider, "After the WTO Protest in Seattle, It's Time to Go on the Offensive. Here's How," *The Nation*, January 31, 2000.

94. Daniel T. Griswold, *Willing Workers: Fixing the Problem of Illegal Mexican Migration to the United States* (Washington, DC: The Cato Institute, 2002).

CHAPTER 8: A COMPACT WITH WORKING AMERICANS

1. Lawrence Mishel, Jared Bernstein, and Heather Boushey, *The State of Working America 2002–2003* (Ithaca, NY: Cornell University

Press, 2003); Edith Rasell, Jared Bernstein, and Heather Boushey, *Step Up, Not Out: The Case for Raising the Federal Minimum Wage for Workers in Every State*, Issue Brief #149, February 7, 2001, Economic Policy Institute; Isabel Sawhill and Adam Thomas, *A Hand Up for the Bottom Third: Toward a New Agenda for Low-Income Working Families*, Brookings Institution, 2001.

2. Jared Bernstein, Heather Boushey, Elizabeth McNichol, and Robert Zahradnik, *Pulling Apart: A State-by-State Analysis of Income Trends*, Center on Budget and Policy Priorities and Economic Policy Institute, April 2002.

3. It could be tied to the median wage or to the growth rate of the nominal average hourly wages for production and nonsupervisory employees.

4. Sawhill and Thomas, *A Hand Up for the Bottom Third*; Jared Bernstein and John Schmitt, *The Impact of the Minimum Wage: Policy Lifts Wages, Maintains Floor for Low-wage Labor Market*, June 2000, Briefing Paper, Economic Policy Institute.

5. Bernstein and Schmitt, *The Impact of the Minimum Wage*.

6. Ibid.

7. David Card and Alan Krueger, "Minimum Wages and Employment: A Case Study of the Fast-Food Industry in New Jersey and Pennsylvania," *American Economic Review*, Vol. 84, No. 4, September 1994; David Card, "Do Minimum Wages Reduce Employment? A Case Study of California, 1987–89," *Industrial and Labor Relations Review*, October 1992; David Card and Alan Krueger, "A Reanalysis of the Effect of the New Jersey Minimum Wage Increase on the Fast-Food Industry with Representative Payroll Data," January 1998, WP#393, Princeton University; David Card and Alan Krueger, *Myth and Measurement: The New Economics of the Minimum Wage* (Princeton, NJ: Princeton University Press, 1995); David Card, "Using Regional Variation in Wages to Measure the Effects of the Federal Minimum Wage," *Industrial and Labor Relations Review*, Vol. 46,

No. 1, 1992, 22–37; Sawhill and Thomas, *A Hand Up for the Bottom Third.*

8. Jared Bernstein, *The Low-Wage Labor Market: Trends and Policy Implications,* Written for the Penn State University 2002 National Symposium on Family, Economic Policy Institute 2002; and see Jared Bernstein and Dean Baker, *The Benefits of Full Employment and the Costs of Not Being There* (Washington, DC: Economic Policy Institute, forthcoming) for an in-depth discussion of the impact of full employment on the lower end of the labor market.

9. While the income of the top 1 percent of taxpayers grew by 59 percent from 1995–1999, those at the bottom half grew by 9 percent. Thus while full employment gave lower-wage workers bargaining power they did not have in a slacker economy, it did not correct the structural inequities in our society. Mishel, et al., *The State of Working America 2002–2003.*

10. Like the military child care system that linked funding to increased spending on workers' wages and benefits.

11. Jared Bernstein, *The Living Wage Movement: What is it, Why is it, and Can it Help?,* Economic Policy Institute, 1999.

12. *Living Wage Ordinances "Stats at a Glance,"* compiled by ACORN, March 2001 http://www.livingwagecampaign.org/Statsataglance3-01.htm.

13. Gene Korez, "The Case for Living-Wage Laws," *Business Week,* April 22, 2002.

14. Bernstein, *The Living Wage Movement.*

15. Greg LeRoy, Fiona Hsu, and Sara Hinkley, *The Policy Shift to Good Jobs: Cities, States, and Counties Attaching Job Quality Standard to Development Subsidies* (Washington, DC: Institute on Taxation and Economic Policy, May 2000). See listing of jurisdictions and kinds of requirements attached to subsidies. At least nine states have passed laws demanding a detailed accounting of subsidies meted out to private industry and provisions that require companies to return the

money if they don't hold up their end of the deals—so-called "claw-backs." Some have attached job-quality standards to these public monies.

16. Greg LeRoy, *Reforming Economic Development: An Enduring Growing Movement*, Neighborhood Founders Group Reports Issue 2, Vol. 7, Summer 2000. A study of incentives in Minnesota found that 72 percent of subsidized jobs paid below average for their corresponding industries; see Greg Leroy and Tyson Slocum, *Economic Development in Minnesota*, Institute on Taxation and Economic Policy, February 1999 at http://www.ctj.org/html/minmeny.htm; Monte Hanson, "Legislature Puts Clamps on Corporate Welfare," *Finance and Commerce*, May 20, 1999.

17. Rachel Duran, "The End of the Candy Store? Many Communities Tie Job Quality Standards to Incentives," *Business Xpansion Journal*, September 2000. See also Greg LeRoy, *No More Candy Store: States and Cities Making Job Subsidies Accountable*, FIRR and Grassroots Policy Project, 1994; LeRoy, et al., *The Policy Shift to Good Jobs*. See listing of jurisdictions and kinds of requirements attached to subsidies.

18. Robert Greenstein and Isaac Shapiro, *New Research Findings on the Effects of the Earned Income Tax Credit*, Center on Budget and Policy Priorities, March 11, 1998.

19. Barry Bluestone and Teresa Ghilarducci, *Making Work Pay: Wage Insurance For the Working Poor*, Jerome Levy Economics Institute of Bard College, Public Policy Brief No. 28, 1996.

20. Daniel N. Shaviro, "Effective Marginal Tax Rates On Low-Income Households," Working Paper, 2001 (http://papers.ssrn.com/sal3/papers.cfm?abstract ids162569).

21. Bluestone and Ghilarducci, *Making Work Pay*.

22. Ibid.

23. Greenstein and Shapiro, *New Research Findings on the Effects of the Earned Income Tax Credit*.

24. Ibid.; Jared Bernstein, "Two Cheers for the EITC," *The American Prospect*, June 19–July 3, 2000.

25. Greenstein and Shapiro, *New Research Findings on the Effects of the Earned Income Tax Credit*.

26. Ibid.

27. Nicholas Johnson, *A Hand Up: How State Earned Income Tax Credits Help Working Families Escape Poverty in 2000: An Overview*, Center on Budget and Policy Priorities, November 2, 2000.

28. Max Sawickey of the Economic Policy Institute suggests a Universal Unified Child Credit combines dependent exemption, child credit, and EITC into single credit that would initially rise along with earnings and then phase down to a minimum benefit of $1,270 per child for all families. Heidi Hartmann suggests combining EITC, dependent deduction, and Child Tax Credit into a Universal Unified Tax Credit that would initially rise with earnings and then phase out. These would be steps toward a family allowance, which would recognize the importance of child rearing and the financial burden imposed in raising a child. Low-income parents would receive a disproportionate share. Heidi Hartmann and Vicky Lovell, "Low-Wage Work is a Women's Issue," paper presented at Domestic Strategy Group of Aspen Institute, 2001.

29. Ellen O'Brien and Judith Feder, "How Well Does the Employment-Based Health Insurance System Work for Low-Income Families?," issue paper, Kaiser Commission on Medicare and the Uninsured, Washington, DC, September 1988.

30. Elliot K. Wicks and Jack A. Meyer, *Prospects for a Reduction in the Number of Uninsured Americans, Covering America: Real Remedies for the Uninsured*, An Economic and Social Research Institute Occasional Paper, December 2001.

31. Richard Kronick and Todd Gilmer, "Explaining the Decline in Health Insurance Coverage, 1979–1995," *Health Affairs*, March/April 1999, Vol. 18, No. 2, 45.

32. Johnson & Johnson already provides a family-care absence that allows an employee time off with pay to provide emergency care for a family member or for a parent-teacher conference.

33. California adopted legislation requiring that employers who give sick leave must allow employees to use one-half of that leave to care for sick family members.

34. Jacques Steinberg, "Gains Found for the Poor in Rigorous Preschool," *The New York Times,* May 9, 2001.

35. Janet Gornick and Marcia K. Meyers, "Support for Working Families—What the U.S. Can Learn from Europe," *The American Prospect,* January 1–15, 2001.

36. Eileen Applebaum, Thomas Bailey, Peter Berg, and Arne Kalleberg, "Shared Work/Valued Care: New Norms for Organizing Market Work and Unpaid Care Work," IRRA Meetings, January 2001.

37. *Maternity Protection at Work,* International Labor Organization, 1997.

38. According to public opinion survey, "What Grown-Ups Understand about Child Development: A National Benchmark Survey," conducted by DYG, Inc. for Zero to Three: The National Center for Infants, Toddlers and Families, Civitas and the Brio Corp; "Maternity Protection at Work," International Labor Organization, 1997.

39. Vicky Lovell and Heidi Hartmann, "Increasing Economic Security for Low-Wage Women Workers," in Richard Kazis and Marc S. Miller, eds., *Low-Wage Workers in the New Economy* (Washington, DC: Urban Institute Press, 2001).

40. *Labor News for Working Families,* Publication of Labor Project for Working Families, Vol. VI, Issue 2, Spring 1998.

41. Elaine McCrate, *Working Mothers in a Double Bind: Working Moms, Minorities Have the Most Rigid Schedules, and Are Paid Less for the Sacrifice,* Economic Policy Institute, Briefing Paper, 2002.

42. Gornick and Meyers, "Support for Working Families—What the U.S. Can Learn from Europe."

43. Barbara Bergmann, "Decent Child Care at Decent Wages," *The American Prospect*, January 1–15, 2001.

44. David M. Blau, *Child Care Subsidy Programs*, NBER Working Paper Series (Cambridge, MA: NBER, July 2000) in which there is a good analysis of a variety of proposals for a universal child-care program.

45. Harriet B. Presser and Amy G. Cox, "The Work Schedules of Low-Educated American Women and Welfare Reform," *Monthly Labor Review* 120(4): 25–34, 1997.

46. Nancy Duff Campbell, Judith Appelbaum, Karin Martinson, and Emily Martin, *Be All That We Can Be: Lessons from the Military for Improving our Nation's Child Care System*, National Women's Law Center, April 2000, 15–16.

47. Some people also refer to this credit as the Child and Dependent Care Tax Credit (CDCTC); Bergmann, "Decent Child Care at Decent Wages."

48. Isabel V. Sawhill, *Investing in Children*, Children's Roundtable Report #1, April 1999.

49. Jonathan Cohn, "Child's Play," *The American Prospect*, June 19–July 3, 2000; Sawhill, *Investing in Children*.

50. Sawhill, *Investing in Children*.

51. Oklahoma provides a universal program in which parents may opt out of the program.

52. Rima Shore, *Our Basic Dream: Keeping Faith with America's Working Families and their Children*, Foundation for Child Development, October 2000.

53. Sawhill, *Investing in Children*.

54. David Ellwood, *The Next Generation of Training and Mobility Strategies for Less Skilled Adult Workers: What Do We Know, What Could the Domestic Strategy Group Do?*, paper presented to the Domestic Strategy Group, Aspen Institute, 2000.

55. *Helping Low-Wage Workers Succeed through Innovative Union Partnerships,* Working for America Institute, April 2002.

56. The San Francisco Hotels Partnership Project, created in 1994, involves twelve unionized first-class hotels and two of the city's largest union locals. The primary goals include: increased market share for participating hotels, retention and improvement of jobs and job security, and new programs for employee involvement, training, and career development. A joint steering committee controls funds from state training agencies and employer contributions.

57. Jay Walljasper, "A Quest for Jobs in San Antonio," *The Nation,* July 21, 1997.

58. Ibid.; Paul Osterman, and Brenda Lautch, Study for Ford Foundation, 1996; Paul Osterman, Thomas A. Kochan, Richard M. Locke, and Michael J. Piore, *Working in America: A Blueprint for the New Labor Market* (Cambridge, MA: MIT Press, 2001).

59. Peggy Clark and Steve L. Dawson, *Jobs and the Urban Poor: Privately Initiated Sectoral Strategies,* The Aspen Institute, Washington, DC, 1995.

60. Michael Grunwald, "A Quiet Crisis in Housing Prices," *The Washington Post,* March 6, 2000.

61. Elizabeth Becker, "Housing Group Calls for More Lower-Cost Rentals," *The New York Times,* March 14, 2001.

62. Ed Lazere, Shawn Fremstad and Heidi Goldberg, *States and Counties are Taking Steps to Help Low-Income Working Families Make Ends Meet and Move Up the Economic Ladder,* Center for Budget and Policy Priorities, May 18, 2001.

63. U.S. Conference of Mayors, "A Status Report on Hunger and Homelessness in America 2000," ii; National Coalition for the Homeless, *How Many People Experience Homelessness,* NCH Fact Sheet #2, February 1999 and *Who is Homeless?* NCH Fact Sheet #3, February 1999; Holly Sklar, Laryssa Mykyta, and Susan Wefald, *Raise the Floor: Wages and Policies That Work for All of Us* (New York: Ms. Foundation for Women, 2001).

64. Sklar, et al., *Raise the Floor.*

65. Ibid.

66. National Research Council and Institute of Medicine, *Musculoskeletal Disorders and the Workplace: Low Back and Upper Extremities* (Washington, DC: National Academy Press, 2001).

67. And 10 percent of all lost time work-related MSDs in the U.S. in 1999 were nursing aides, orderlies, and attendants, along with registered nurses. Sixty-five percent of injuries and illnesses involving days away from work for nursing aides, orderlies, and attendants are due to sprains and strains. Workers in meat packing plants have a repetitive trauma disorder incidence rate of 912 per 10,000 full-time workers.

68. National Research Council and Institute of Medicine, *Musculoskeletal Disorders and the Workplace.*

69. Ibid.

70. U.S. General Accounting Office, *Worker Protection: Private Sector Ergonomics Programs Yield Positive Results* GAO/hehs-97-163 (Washington, DC: U.S. General Accounting Office, 1997).

71. U.S. Department of Labor, Occupational Safety and Health Administration, "Incidence rates of nonfatal occupational injuries" and Bureau of Labor Statistics, "Workplace Injuries and Illnesses," annual reports.

72. U.S. General Accounting Office, *Unemployment Insurance: Role as Safety Net for Low-Wage Workers is Limited,* GAO-01-181 (Washington, DC: U.S. General Accounting Office, December 2000).

73. Even if low-wage workers qualify for unemployment insurance, there is a time lag between the time they apply and the time they receive compensation. The time allotted in many states for processing wage records may require that a claimant wait between three and six months before receiving benefits to which he or she is entitled. U.S. General Accounting Office, *Unemployment Insurance.*

74. Ibid.

75. Maurice Enselem, Jessica Goldberg, Rick McHugh, Wendell Primus, Rebecca Smith, and Jeffrey Wenger, *Failing the Unemployed*

(Washington, DC: Economic Policy Institute and Center on Budget and Policy Priorities; New York: National Employment Law Project, March 2002); Paul Osterman, *Securing Prosperity: The American Labor Market: How It Has Changed and What to Do About It* (Princeton, NJ: Princeton University Press, 1999); National Employment Law Project, *Women, Low-Wage Workers and the Unemployment Compensation System: State Legislative Models for Change* (New York: National Employment Law Project, October 1997).

76. Alicia H. Munnell and Annika Sunden, *Private Pensions: Coverage and Benefit Trends,* paper prepared for "Conversation on Coverage" Conference, Washington, DC, July 24–25, 2001.

77. Munnell and Sunden, *Private Pensions.*

78. Pension Rights Center, Washington, DC, "Conversation on Coverage," website at http://www.pensioncoverage.net/Andrews.htm.

79. Teresa Ghilarducci, "Rising Expectations: Women, Retirement Security, and Private Pensions," in Sheldon Friedman and David C. Jacobs, eds., Industrial Relations Research Association Series, *The Future of the Safety Net: Social Insurance and Employee Benefits* (Ithaca, NY: Cornell University Press, 2001).

80. Lance Compa, *Unfair Advantage: Workers' Freedom of Association in the United States Under International Human Rights Standards* (New York: Human Rights Watch, 2000).

81. One way of dealing with the bargaining delays upon certification is to make the National Labor Relations Act self-enforcing.

82. *ILO Declaration On Fundamental Principles and Rights At Work and Its Follow-Up: Adopted by the International Labour Conference at its Eighty-Sixth Session, Geneva, 18 June 1998, Congressional Record,* June 23, 1998; *International Worker Rights—A Human Face for the Global Economy, a Report by the United Nations Association of the United States of America,* National Capital Area Task Force on Worker Rights in the Global Economy, November 1999.

83. *ILO Declaration On Fundamental Principles and Rights At*

Work and Its Follow-Up: Adopted by the International Labour Confer-ence at its Eighty-Sixth Session.

84. Ibid. See also the Universal Declaration of Human Rights of 1948 that covers a wide range of issues, including many that specifi-cally relate to workers' rights. For example, Article 20 declares that "Everyone has the right to freedom of peaceful assembly and associa-tion" and Article 23 declares that "Everyone has the right to work, to free choice of employment, to just and favorable conditions of work, and to protections against unemployment. . . . Everyone, without any discrimination, has the right to equal pay for equal work. . . . Every-one who works has the right to just and favorable remuneration ensur-ing for himself and his family an existence worthy of human dignity, and supplemented, if necessary, by other means of social protection. . . . Everyone has the right to form and join trade unions for the pro-tection of his interests."

85. "Shaping Globalization After Seattle," *ILO Focus,* Spring 2000, 3, speech before the World Trade Organization in Seattle.

86. Ibid.

87. See for example, Section 301 of the Trade Act of 1974, which states that the United States Trade Representative is authorized to "suspend, withdraw, or prevent the application of benefits of trade agreement concessions" to any country that "(i) denies workers the right of association, (ii) denies workers the right to organize and bar-gain collectively, (iii) permits any form of forced or compulsory labor, (iv) fails to provide a minimum age for the employment of children, or (v) fails to provide standards for minimum wages, hours of work, and occupational safety and health of workers." The law, which ap-plies to all U.S. trading partners, provides a broad range of sanctions, from setting a higher tariff on a single product, company, or industry, to removal of the entire country's trade preferences.

88. D'Vera Cohn, "Immigrants Account for Half of New Work-ers," *The Washington Post,* December 2, 2002.

89. Daniel T. Griswold, *Willing Workers: Fixing the Problem of Illegal Mexican Migration to the United States* (Washington, DC: The Cato Institute, 2002).

90. See former House Minority Leader Dick Gephardt's proposed legislation that provides earned legalization to undocumented immigrants who have resided here for five years, worked here for two years, and have played by the rules. Speech before the National Council of La Raza, Miami Beach, July 22, 2002, http://democraticleader.house. gov/media/speeches/readSpeech,asp? ID58.

91. Christopher Howard, *The Hidden Welfare State: Tax Expenditures and Social Policy in the United States* (Princeton, NJ: Princeton University Press, 1997).

92. Donald L. Barlett and James B. Steele, "Corporate Welfare," *Time,* November 9, 1998; Donald L. Bartlett and James B. Steele, "Fantasy Islands and Other Perfectly Legal Ways that Big Companies Manage to Avoid Billions in Federal Taxes," *Time,* November 16, 1998.

INDEX

absenteeism, 93–94

ACORN, 143

advancement opportunities, 72–73,
   102–103

Advisory Committee on Student
   Financial Assistance, 88

AFL-CIO, 140

African-Americans, 15–18, 70, 76, 108
   family disintegration, 91
   see also minority workers

airline workers, 50–53, 127

airport security, 12, 95, 96

air traffic controllers, 130–31

alcoholism, 92

American Federation of State, County,
   and Municipal Employees
   (AFSCME), 145, 167

American University, 74

"apartheid economy," 7

Appleseed, 143

Avondale shipyard, 134

"bad jobs," 10
   to "good jobs," 122–24

Baltimoreans United in Leadership
   Development (BUILD), 145

banking industry, 128

Barry, Barbara, 41

before- and after-school programs,
   165

benefits, employee:
   lack of, 7–8
   for low-wage workers, 35
   for part-time workers, 32–33
   shareholder wealth and, 129
   unemployment, 42–44, 138
   unionization and, 123–24, 135

Bernstein, Aaron, 133

Beverly Enterprises, 146
Bible, vi
black market in labor, 147
Bluestone, Barry, 155–56
Boston College, 102
Breslin Learning Center, 167
Bright, Sharon, 53–55
Bronfenbrenner, Kate, 126
Bronx, New York, 169–70
Brookings Institution, 111–12
Brown University, 146
Bureau of Labor Statistics, 172
Bush, George H. W., 173
Bush, George W., 112
Business Roundtable, 146, 147
Business Week, 133, 137
Butler, Bob, 21–23, 27, 58

call-center workers, 6, 31
    described, 50–53
    globalization and, 110
    skills for, 107
    working conditions for, 39–40
Capelli, Peter, 136
career ladders, 102–103, 166–67
Care for the Caregivers Alabama
    Campaign, 146
carpal tunnel syndrome, 118, 172–73
cashiers, 105, 106
casino industry, 141
caste system, 12
    basics of, 69–71
    demography of, 69–79

catfish workers, 6
Cato Institute, 147
Chamber of Commerce, 146
changed economy, 149
charities, 112–13, 114
child care, 8, 113, 115
    access to, 163–66
    cost of, 36–37, 74, 163
    low-income families and, 85
    by parents, 34–37
    subsidies, 84–85
    substandard, 85
Child Care and Development Fund,
    164–65
child-care workers, 6, 13
    described, 53–55
    turnover rates of, 96, 164
    wages of, 55, 72, 163
children, costs of low-wage jobs to,
    82–89
    education of, 85–88
    equal opportunity and, 83–86
    family care, 87
    government subsidies, 84–85
    health issues, 86
    poverty rates, 82–83, 156
    society, 88–89
    strong correlations, 84
Children's Defense Fund, 144
Children's Health Insurance Program
    (CHIP), 27, 86
Child Tax Credit, 157
Clinton, Bill, 104, 177

coalitions of concerned Americans, 140–47
  consumers, 146
  family and child advocacy groups, 144
  living wage groups, 143–44
  religious community, 144–45
  socially responsible corporations, 146–47
  students, 145–46
  unions, 140–43
  women, 144
COBRA, 43
collective bargaining, 10–11
  legal rights and, 122–24, 178–79
  see also unions
Columbia University, 75, 83
communities, costs of low-wage jobs to, 91–93
Compact with Working Americans, 13–14, 149–84
  affordable and safe housing, 170–71
  affordable health care, 158–60
  child care/early education, 163–66
  Child Tax Credit, 157
  conclusion, 182–84
  Earned Income Tax Credit, 155–56
  eliminate pay inequities, 157–58
  goal of full employment, 152
  immigration policies, 181–82
  introduction, 149
  job flexibility, 160–62

  opportunity to gain new skills, 166–70
  paid family and medical leave, 162–63
  public dollars reflecting public values, 152–55
  purpose, 149
  raise and index the minimum wage, 150–52
  retirement benefits, 176–78
  right to organize and collectively bargain, 178–79
  safe and healthy working environment, 171–73
  sufficient income to meet a family's basic needs, 150–58
  summary, 150
  trade policies, 180–81
  unemployment benefits, 174–76
computer-based jobs, 106
conservatism, 83, 111
consumable goods and services, 94
Consumer Federation of America, 146
consumer groups, 146
consumers, costs of low-wage jobs to, 95–98
Consumers Union, 146
Cooperative Home Care Associates (CHCA), 97, 169–70
"core worker rights," 180–81
Cornell University, 126
corporate-employee relationship, 129
corporate policy, 11

corporate subsidies, 154
corporate welfare, 183
Corporations for Social Responsibility,
    147
cost of living, 151, 153
costs of low-wage jobs, 81–100
    to children, 82–89
    to communities, 91–93
    to consumers, 95–98
    to democracy, 89–90
    to families, 90–91
    introduction, 81–82
    to our economy, 93–95
    to our nation's health, 98–100
Craig, Earl, 38–39
credit, 28
crime, 28, 84, 92–93, 115
Culinary Training Academy, 141, 168
Culinary Workers Union, 141, 168
cut backs, 33–34

Danziger, Sheldon, 102
democracy, costs of low-wage jobs to,
    89–90
Democratic Party, 130, 136
Dependent Care Tax Credit (DCTC),
    164–65
deregulation of industries, 125, 127
dignity, 41–42
discrimination, 71, 76, 136–37, 157,
    174, 175
District 1199C, 167
divorce, 37, 90

"doing the right thing," 13
Dole, Elizabeth, 173
"dot" system, 36
downsizing, 125, 129
drug addiction, 92, 113, 115
dual-earner couples, 37

Earned Income Tax Credit (EITC),
    155–56
economic costs of low-wage jobs,
    93–95
economic downturns, 94, 121
Economic Policy Institute, 27, 154
education, 8
    children and, 85–88, 163–66
    college, 50, 71, 87–88
    demographics of, 69–71, 76
    employer-sponsored, 42, 93, 128,
        166–70
    immigrant workers and, 78
    job opportunities linked to, 166–70
    skills and, 104, 107–108
    workplace, 105, 108
Ehrenreich, Barbara, 7
Ellwood, David, 93
emergency food assistance, 114
emergency-room care, 31, 86
"equal opportunity," 83–86, 108,
    124
equity and fairness, 81–82, 90, 93–95
    see also Compact with Working
        Americans
ergonomic injuries, 118, 172–73

European workers, 26, 73–74, 82, 103, 111, 161
evening/night shifts, 34, 37
eviction, 27–28
exploitation, 4–14

Fair Labor Standards Act, 33
Fairley, Bill, 132–33
faith-based voluntary solutions, 112–15, 144–45
families, costs of low-wage jobs to, 90–91
Families USA, 144
family and child advocacy groups, 144
Family and Medical Leave Act (FMLA), 33, 35, 36, 74, 144, 161–62
"family gap," 75
family leave, 34–35, 74–75
    job flexibility and, 160–61
    paid, 160–63
fast-food jobs, 45
fear, 8
Federal Part-Time Career Employment Act, 161
Federal Reserve, 125, 128
female workers, 7, 55
    advancement opportunities for, 72–73
    demographics of, 69–75
    "female" jobs, 72–75, 157, 161
    minimum wage of, 137–38

part-time and temporary employment of, 73
single mothers, 36
as sole support of the family, 75
working mothers, 73–75
with young children, 161–63
flextime, 35, 75, 160–61
food banks, 113, 114
food-processing jobs, 105, 110
food stamps, 6, 27
Fortin, Nicole M., 130
401(K) plans, 177–78
Freeman, Richard, 7, 92, 139
full employment, 128, 152

Galbraith, James, 122, 128
gap between haves and have nots, 12, 83, 99
garment industry workers, 79
gender issues:
    demographics of, 69–79
    part-time work, 32–33
    see also female workers
George and Stanley's, 16, 17
Georgia, 165
Ghilarducci, Teresa, 155–56
globalization, 109–12
    basic human values and, 180–81
    shift in worker power and, 125–29
"good jobs," 10
    from "bad jobs" to, 122–24
Gottschalk, Peter, 102

government regulation, 10–11
    funding for agencies, 139
    influence and, 89–90
    temporary workers and, 33
government subsidies, 84–85
Great Depression, 122–24
Griswold, Daniel T., 147
grocery store industry, 38–39
gross domestic product, 94
guest room attendant, 63–65

"hamburger flippers," 46
H&R Block, 16
Harrington, Michael, 4, 184
Hartmann, Heidi, 73
Harvard University, 7, 91, 92, 93, 99,
    133, 139, 146
hazardous working conditions, 37–41
    elimination of, 171–73
health:
    of children, 86
    costs of national, 98–100
Health Facilities Association of
    Maryland, 97
health insurance, 29–31, 113, 146
    affordable, 158–60
    children and, 86
    costs of, 30
    emergency-room care and, 31, 86
    employer provided, 29, 159
    lack of, 29–31, 114, 158
    layoffs and, 42–43
    for part-time workers, 157–58

qualification for, 86
    sick pay and, 31
    smaller firms and, 29–30
    subsidies for, 158
    unions and, 135
heart of our economy, low-wage jobs
    in, 45–68
    call-center workers, 50–53
    child-care workers, 53–55
    guest room attendant, 63–65
    home health-care workers, 60–63
    human-relation skills and, 46
    introduction, 45–46
    janitors, 55–57
    labeling and, 46
    pharmacy technical assistant,
        65–67
    poultry-processing workers, 57–60
    receptionist, 67–68
    service sector, 47–50
    types of jobs, 45–46
Heckman, James, 83–84
Heffernan, William, 78–79
higher education, 166
higher-income jobs, 48, 75
    child care and, 164
High Performance Incentive Program
    (HPIP), 155
high school graduates, 135
high-tech jobs, 104–106
holidays and vacations, 35
Holland, Nancy, 67–68
Holzer, Harry J., 76

home health-care workers, 5–6, 13,
    105
  described, 60–63
  education of, 169–70
  organizing of, 140
  quality of service and, 96, 97
  skills of, 107
  working conditions for, 39
homeless shelters, 113, 114
hopelessness, 113
Horatio Alger myth, 102
hotel workers, 6, 13
  described, 63–65
  education of, 168
  unionization of, 141
  working conditions for, 40
housing, 28
  access to affordable and safe,
    170–71
human-relations skills, 46, 106–107
Human Rights Watch, 132, 134

"ideal worker," 74
immigrant workers, 7, 72, 144
  English proficiency of, 78
  fair treatment of, 181–82
  globalization and, 125–27
  likely jobs of, 77–78
  as lowest of low-wage workers,
    76–79
  socially-responsible corporations
    and, 146–47
  statistics on, 77, 127

undocumented, 77–79, 181–82
  unions and, 178–79
incarceration, 92–93
indifference, 101–15
individual responsibility, 113–14
Industrial Areas Foundation, 143
industrialized countries, 26, 73–74, 82,
    103, 111, 161
inflation, 125, 128
In-Home Supportive Services, 140
injuries, 34–41
  being fired because of, 41
  elimination of, 171–73
Institute for Women's Policy
    Research, 73
Institute of Medicine, 172
International Labour Organization
    (ILO), 112, 180–81
International Monetary Fund, 181
investment in workers, 93

janitorial workers, 6, 13, 105
  described, 55–57
  unionization of, 141–42
  wages of, 57
job growth, 49–50
job quality standards, 155
Jobs with Justice, 143
Johns Hopkins University, 146
Joint Center for Poverty Research,
    84
Jones, Bill, 42
Justice for Janitors Campaign, 141

Kane, Rosalie, 97–98
Kansas, 155
Katz, Lawrence, 139
Kawachi, Ichiro, 99
Kennedy, Bruce, 99
Kessell Food Store, 15, 17
Klein, Donna, 98
Kochan, Thomas, 132
Kroger, 17
Krueger, Alan, 96
Krugman, Paul, 112
Ku Klux Klan, 118

labor laws, 11, 124
lateness, 35
Latinos, 18–21, 70, 76, 78, 108
    in poultry processing plants,
        117–21
    see also minority workers
Lemieux, Thomas, 130
less-developed countries, 109, 125,
    129
Levy, Frank, 95
liberalism, 130
    refocused agenda of, 136–37
libertarianism, 84
Litton Industries, 134
living wage coalitions, 143–44, 145
living-wage ordinances, 143, 145
    public money and, 153, 154
Lovell, Vicky, 73
low-road policies, 93–95
"low-skill" jobs, 8–9

low-wage jobs:
    characteristics of, 25
    costs of, *see* costs of low-wage jobs
    decline in pay for, 26
    defined, 25*n*
    demographics of, 69–79, 94
    dignity and, 41–42
    evening/night shifts, 34
    eviction and, 27–28
    family care and, 34–37
    health insurance and, *see* health
        insurance
    in the heart of our economy, *see*
        heart of our economy, low-wage
        jobs in
    labeling of, 46, 106–107
    making ends meet, 25–29
    myths of, *see* myths
    new economy and, 105–106
    in other industrialized countries,
        26, 73–74, 103, 111, 161
    part-time, 32–34
    poverty level and, 25–27
    safety issues and, 37–41
    security and, 42–44
    standard of living and, 26, 27
    tight labor market and, 94, 121,
        127

making ends meet, 25–29
manufacturing sector:
    decline of, 47
    globalization and, 109–10, 125–29

during the 1930s and 1940s, 122–24

skills and, 104–105

unionization of, 10, 11

wages in, 49

women and, 75

market failure, 83–84, 95

marriage rates, 90–91

Marriott International, 98

Martin, Lynn, 173

Maryland General Assembly, 96–97

maternity leave, 36, 74

maximizing shareholder value, 125, 129, 147

meat industry workers, 60, 79, 139, 143

Medicaid, 27, 86, 153, 158, 159–60

Medicare, 153, 155, 158, 159

Mexico, 126

Michigan State University, 154

middle-income jobs:

child care and, 164

decline of, 105

in manufacturing, 47

in service sector, 48

Military Child Care Act, 164

Milwaukee, Wisconsin, 168–69

minimum wage:

first federal, 124

part-time work and, 32

raising and indexing, 150–52

as reference point, 137

undercutting of, 137–38

Minnesota, 154–55

minority workers, 7, 16

case histories, 15–21

demographics of, 69–79

unions and, 117–21

Mirage hotels, 98

MIT, 95, 112, 132

mobility myth, 101–103

monetary policy, 11

morality, 81–82, 95

Morris, Joann, 60–62

multiple jobs, 37

musculoskeletal disorders (MSDs), 118, 172–73

myths, 101–15

globalization, 109–12

introduction, 101

mobility, 101–103

reskilling, 103–109

volunteerism, 112–15

Nathan, Artie, 98

National Academy of Arbitrators, 131

National Academy of Sciences, 172

national health, costs of low-wage jobs to, 98–100

National Immigrant Forum, 146–47

National Interfaith Committee for Worker Justice, 145

National Labor Relations Act, 33, 122–23, 131–32

National Labor Relations Board (NLRB), 21, 132–33, 134, 178, 179

National Low Income Housing
Coalition, 170
National Partnership for Women and
Families, 144
National Research Council, 172
*National Study for the Changing
Workforce*, 93
National Union of Hospital and
Health Care Employees, 167
Nelson, Ellen, 50–53
Neumark, David, 154
New Deal, 10, 136–37
"new economy," 48, 105–106
New York Times, The, 85
*Nickel and Dimed: On (Not) Getting
By in America* (Ehrenreich), 7
North American Commission for
Labor Cooperation, 126
North American Free Trade
Agreement (NAFTA), 126
Northeastern University, 155
Northwestern University, 84
Notre Dame University, 156
nurse's aides, 39, 62–63
nursing home workers, 1–3, 5–6,
132
    coalitions to aid, 146
    described, 62–63
    dignity issue and, 41
    government subsidies and, 153
    health insurance for, 30
    mandatory overtime for, 36
    quality of service and, 96–97

Occupational Safety and Health
Administration (OSHA), 139,
171–72, 173
occupational segregation, 72
"occurrences," 31
Oklahoma, 165
on-the-job training, 105, 108
OPEC, 128
Organization for Economic
Cooperation and Development
(OECD), 74, 103
Other America, The (Harrington), 4
overtime, 36, 124

part-time jobs, 32–34
    as "female" jobs, 73, 157, 161
    pay inequities of, 157–58
pay inequities, 157–58
pension plans, 43–44
    expansion of, 176–78
    part-time workers and, 157–58
personal consumption, 94
pharmacy technical assistant,
65–67
Phelps, Edmund, 83
Philadelphia employment-training
initiative, 167–68
Phillips, Peter, 91
"pin money," 75
politics, 9, 11
    "bad" jobs to "good" jobs and,
122–24
    globalization and, 110–12

ideological shift, 125–31, 137
money and, 89–90
relative wages and, 121–22
unions and, 130–31
worker skills and, 107
Porter, Cynthia, 1–3, 5, 27, 28, 30, 33, 36, 39, 41, 42, 89, 132, 136
poultry processing workers, 6, 13
case history, 21–23
described, 57–60
globalization and, 126
working conditions for, 37–38, 117–21, 139
poverty, 4
poverty level, 25–27, 55
bypassing the official, 27, 82–83
of children, 82–83, 156
minimum wage and, 150–52
public money and, 153
power, 117–47
anti-union, 117–21
from "bad" jobs to "good" jobs, 122–24
challenging the imbalance of, 140–47
consumer groups and, 146
of employers, 131–34
family and child advocacy groups and, 144
immigrants' lack of, 117–21
living wage coalitions and, 143–44, 145
minimum wage and, 137–38

most vulnerable workers and, 130–39
politics and, 121–22
religious community and, 144–45
shift in worker, 125–29
socially responsible corporations and, 146–47
student groups and, 145–46
unionization and, 122–24, 130–43
women's groups and, 144
preschool, 165
prime labor force, 93
Princeton University, 96, 112
productivity, 93
Progressive Policy Institute, 111–12
Project Quest, 143, 169
PTA activities, 35
public dollars reflecting public values, 152–55
purchasing power, 94

quality of service, 96–98

railroad workers, 127
RAND, 165
Reagan, Ronald, 130, 139, 155
real income, 121–22
receptionists, 67–68
Reich, Michael, 96
Reich, Robert, 104
relative wages, 121–22
religious community, 144–45

repetitive motion injuries, 38, 118, 172–73
Republican Party, 173
reskilling myth, 103–109
"responsible labor relations," 153–54
retail food workers, 11, 124
    case history, 15–18
retail store workers, 6, 110
    described, 65–67
    wages for, 48–49
    working conditions for, 38–41
retirement benefits, 43–44, 135
    expansion of, 176–78
Rimer, Sara, 85
Ross, Vevia, 40

safety, 8, 21–23, 37–41, 124, 171–73
St. Antoine, Theodore, 131
Salvation Army, 18, 114
Sanchez, Maria, 141
San Francisco International Airport, 96
San Jose, California, 142, 153
Santa Rosa, California, 91
scheduling:
    "deviations," 40
    flexible, 35, 75, 160–61
    of work hours, 35–36
SCHIP, 158, 159–60
Section 8 housing program, 171
security, 42–44
security guards, 107

segmentation of labor, 102–103
Segunda, Flor, 18–21, 27, 28, 30, 37, 55–57, 84, 161
September 11, 12, 95, 96
Service Employees International Union (SEIU), 20–21
    organization activities of, 140–43
service sector, 11–14, 47–50, 110
    components of, 47–48
    expansion of, 47, 49–50
    globalization and, 109
    low-wage jobs in, 48–50
    social contract and, 124
    unions and, 130
severance pay, 42, 174
sick leave, 34, 160
sick pay, 31
Simpson, Dennis, 31, 40
single parents, 36, 91
skills, concept of, 106–107
"skills mismatch," 103–109, 128
slippage, 51
small firms:
    discrimination by, 76
    family leave and, 35
    health insurance and, 29–30
Smith, Adam, vi
Smithfield, Judy, 65–67
social capital, 99
social consciousness, 122
"social contract," 123–24
    elimination of, 125
social legislation, 10–11, 136–39

socially responsible corporations,
    146–47
social policy, 112–15
    see also Compact with Working
        Americans
Social Security, 124, 155, 158, 176–77
Somavia, Juan, 112, 180
Sonoma State University, 91
South Bay Central Labor Council, 142
standard of living, 26
    European, 111
    other family members and, 27
Stanton, Patricia, 39
stereotypes, 8–9
Stevens, Linda, 15–18, 27, 28, 31, 33,
    35–36, 37, 38, 40–41, 43, 84
Stewart, Darlene, 33
stratification, 102–103
stress-related illnesses, 39–40
student groups, 145–46
subsidies, government:
    child care and, 164–65
    public values and, 152–55
supply and demand, 121–22
sweatshops, 40, 145

taxes, 91, 92, 147
    Child Tax Credit, 157
    Dependent Care Tax Credit,
        164–65
    Earned Income Tax Credit, 155–56
    public values and, 152–55
    retirement and, 177–78

teacher's aides, 55
Teamsters Union, 23
technology, 9, 128
teenagers:
    pregnancies by, 91
    as workers, 69
telecommunication industry, 11, 124,
    127
temporary workers, 33
    as "female" jobs, 73
    minorities and, 76
    unionization of, 142–43
Thomas, Mary, 38
threats by employers:
    anti-union, 117–21, 130–35, 179
    globalization and, 110–11, 125–26
3M, 172–73
TIAA-CREF, 177
Together @ Work, 142–43
Tomkins PLC, 126
Trade Adjustment Act, 176
trade policy, 11, 180–81
transportable skills, 110
transportation, 29
Trico Products Corporation, 126
trucking workers, 127
turnover, 54, 55, 62, 93
    costs to consumers of, 96–98

unemployment, 42–44, 138
    full employment versus, 152
    government policies and, 125, 128
    minimum wage and, 152, 154

unemployment insurance (UI), 43,
    135
  extended coverage by, 174–76
  undercutting, 138
unfair labor practices, 132–33
unions, 3, 11, 20–21, 117–47
  benefits and, 135
  decline of, 130–36
  employee education and, 167–69
  globalization and, 125–29
  hardball tactics against, 117–21,
    130–35, 178–79
  industrial deregulation and, 127
  last 25 years, 129–39
  nonunion workers and, 10, 123, 136
  public sector, 134–35
  revitalization of, 140–43
  during the 1930s and 1940s, 122–24
  wages and, 49, 135
United Food and Commercial
    Workers Union, 146
U.S. Conference of Mayors, 114
U.S. Congress, 122, 124, 130, 161,
    164
U.S. Department of Agriculture, 59
U.S. Department of Housing and
    Urban Development (HUD),
    171
U.S. Department of Labor, 79
United Students Against Sweatshops,
    145
"Universal Savings Accounts" (USA),
    177

Université de Montréal, 130
University of California, 96, 145
University of Chicago, 83
University of Michigan, 102, 131
University of Minnesota, 97
University of Missouri, 78
University of Sussex, 99
University of Tennessee-Knoxville,
    146
University of Texas, 122
University of Virginia, 146
utilities, 28

vacation time, 160
Verizon, 40
Vietnam War, 128
volunteerism as social policy,
    112–15
voter turnout, 89–90

wage policy, 11
Waldfogel, Jane, 75
Wal-Mart, 47
Wealth of Nations, The (Smith), vi
Weiler, Paul, 133
welfare, 4, 7, 85
Wesleyan University, 146
Wharton School of Business, 136
whistle-blower protection, 171–72
Wilkinson, Richard, 99
Williams, Joan, 74
Wilson, William Julius, 91

Wisconsin Regional Training
    Partnership (WRTP), 168–69
women, *see* female workers
women's advocacy groups, 144
Work and Family Institute, 93
Working for America, 167
Working Partnerships USA, 142

Working Today, 143–44
Workplace Project, 144
World Bank, 181
World Trade Organization, 112
world wage structure, 110

Xerox, 172